The Dream in Psychoanalysis

THE DREAM IN PSYCHOANALYSIS

Revised Edition

LEON L. ALTMAN, M.D.

INTERNATIONAL UNIVERSITIES PRESS, INC.

NEW YORK

Library of Congress Cataloging in Publication Data

Altman, Leon L   1911-
  The dream in psychoanalysis.

  Bibliography: p.
  Includes indexes.

  1. Dreams.   2. Psychoanalysis.   I. Title
BF1078.A53   1975   616.8'917   75-17258
ISBN 0-8236-1431-X

Second Printing, 1969
Third Printing, 1974
Fourth Printing, 1979

Acknowledgments

My students provided the stimulus for this book; my patients made it possible.

I wish to express my deepest appreciation and thanks to: Dr. Sylvia Brody and Dr. Sidney Axelrad, for helpful advice; Dr. Elise Snyder, for critical comments and assistance with the organization of the book in its formative stages; Miss Liselotte Bendix, Librarian of the New York Psychoanalytic Institute who, while supplying me with references, performed numerous acts of kindness; Dr. Mark Kanzer, for his interest in and scholarly review of the manuscript—he saved me from a number of embarrassing errors of omission and commission and offered useful suggestions; Dr. Charles Fisher, who extended himself to give me his time and expert opinion on substantive matters of dream physiology, went over the manuscript, suggested important emendations, and encouraged me throughout;

ACKNOWLEDGMENTS

Dr. Otto Isakower who, although not responsible for the contents herein, *is* responsible for making me aware of the state of mind we must bring to the dream in order to share it with our patients—I am particularly indebted to him for invaluable suggestions offered after he had read the manuscript; Mrs. Janet K. Schneider for her scrupulous editorial assistance, painstaking reading and rereading of the manuscript in all its stages, and sense of the appropriate in style. I thank my wife, who lived with this book from beginning to end, asked provocative questions, insisted on countless improvements, kept it on earth when I threatened to let it soar into outer space, and kept it alive when I thought it deserved burial.

Contents

The Dream in Psychoanalysis

Introduction

Once upon a time, all psychoanalysts believed with Freud that the interpretation of dreams was "the royal road to a knowledge of the unconscious activities of the mind." Today, reports from many sources suggest that changing times and customs have affected the status of the dream in the clinical practice of psychoanalysis; the dream seems to have fallen into disuse. A considerable number of reputable psychoanalysts regard the dream as a subsidiary clinical instrument. I do not share this attitude. I consider the dream essential to an exploration of the unconscious. I believe that psychoanalysis without embracing the dream is inexact and incomplete.

Current emphasis on ego psychology may have led to diminution of interest in the dream. Years ago, when interest centered on the id, it also centered on the dream. New theoretical formulations of adaptation, identity, psychic energy, and so forth have drawn emphasis away from the id. Perhaps withdrawal of emphasis on the id has resulted in withdrawal of emphasis on the dream and has contributed to relegating the dream to a position of secondary importance. In line with the trend toward ego psychology, the personal analyses of those who have recently completed their formal clinical analytic training may not provide them with the conviction that comes from experiencing their own dreams. No teaching process can substitute for this experience. It is essential to an understanding of the dream's role in psychoanalysis.

Colleagues associated with training institutes around the country report, and my own experience confirms, that many of those recently trained in psychoanalysis do not know what to do with the dream and tend to regard it as a thing apart. We find that, although students and recent graduates may understand dreams easily enough and can translate them from the language of the unconscious into their native tongue, they do not know how to integrate dreams with the problems the patient brings to psychoanalysis. Our theoretical and clinical training evidently leaves something to be desired. My principal goal is to make good this deficiency, to complement the help offered in supervision by describing one psychoanalyst's way of working with the dream. My supplementary aim is to revive interest and enthusiasm for the dream, to reaffirm the extent as well as limitations of its importance in the practice of psychoanalysis, and to help the student by rounding out his experience with my own.

This book is based on Freud's work with the dream, presupposes a familiarity with psychoanalytic method and theory, and is designed for those trained in this discipline.

More specifically, it is meant to be read in conjunction with Freud's major writings on the dream,[1] especially *The Interpretation of Dreams* (1900). In my opinion, it will have its optimal usefulness and be most meaningful to those who are actively concerned with dreams, both patients' and their own.

Psychoanalytic theory of dream psychology has always gone hand in hand with the dream in the clinical practice of psychoanalysis. Advances in clinical understanding have also implemented theoretical knowledge. One cannot be divorced from the other. The first section of this book, therefore, gives a summary review of dream theory and is followed by a more extensive consideration of the dream's clinical and practical application.

The chapter headings in the second section should not be misconstrued. Dreams cannot be categorized, labeled like so many pieces of merchandise. To sort out and make an inventory of dreams would devitalize them. Very few dreams are accommodating enough to arrange themselves for teaching convenience, to limit their content to a topic under scrutiny. I frequently found it difficult to decide whether a particular dream would better illustrate one point or another. Although separation of dreams into categories would be misleading and artificial, this does not invalidate my division of the book into chapters according to the emphasis I thought each dream required in its clinical context.

I regret I have had to sacrifice so much of the richness and subtlety of the analytic hour in order to present the dream examples concisely. Readers with psychoanalytic

[1] See Bibliography, "Basic Readings."

experience may well protest, "But my patients don't come to the point this way." Of course they don't; neither did mine. Considerations of readability demanded that compulsive honesty yield to coherent presentation. Compression of the material inevitably resulted in the sacrifice of nuances so characteristic of psychoanalytic interchange, nuances that often influence our procedures. Dreams do not come in tidy parcels; neither do associations. We regularly wade through oceans of circumlocution to get at the gist of the message. A few dreams were excerpted from longer and more involved productions. I have tampered far less with the dream, however, than with the associations, where discursiveness is the rule. These I have winnowed, sifting out the prolixity, except in a few instances where I believed the interplay between dream and associations so revealing and rewarding that deletion would seriously compromise the meaning of the hour. On the whole, the dream, context, associations, and interventions are given as they occurred.

Each patient, each situation, each dream is unlike any other. Every interpretation of a dream must be custom-tailored, based upon the best evidence available to the analyst at the time. He has to learn from experience how to evaluate and select the essential from a mass of information and impressions. I have tried to show how the analyst goes about making his selection, why he emphasizes one aspect of a dream and not another.

The term "interpretation," as used in the clinical practice of psychoanalysis, actually has two meanings, each of which can be thought of as a phase. The interpretation the analyst makes for himself is one thing; the interpretation he offers the patient is another, and constitutes the paramount activity in analytic therapy. In connection with dreams, interpretation in the first sense—a theoretical formulation —transcribes the manifest content into latent thoughts. Interpretation in the second sense—the clinical interpretation—presents these latent thoughts to the patient in a form he can digest.

This book is concerned with the second phase of interpretation, the clinical, therapeutic one and, presupposing the reader's capacity for the first phase, is only incidentally about the meaning of dreams. It is an exposition of the clinical approach to making the latent content available and meaningful to both patient and analyst—an account of the clinical judgments that must be made and the steps taken to this end.

I hope my readers will find much more in the dreams than I have set forth. To go back to a dream after an interval invariably yields fresh insights, connections, and relationships. Finally, I hope this book will not leave the impression that I think psychoanalysis consists solely of working with the dream. Nothing could be further from the truth.

PART I

THEORETICAL CONSIDERATIONS

1
A Summary Review
of Dream Theory

Freud assigned value to the dream at least ten years before the publication of *The Interpretation of Dreams* (1900). While treating Frau Emmy von N. (Breuer and Freud, 1893-1895), he found she volunteered her dreams along with other descriptive material. Having discovered transference, resistance, and the need for an autonomous ego in therapy, Freud abandoned hypnosis, which created distortions in and added complications to these essential factors, and turned instead to free association and the method we know as psychoanalysis. Freud then used the dream as the starting point for associations which ultimately led to the unconscious ideas hidden behind symptoms and dreams and responsible for both. For the first time, the meaning of dreams was approached scientifically.

Today, we know that to sleep is to dream and "perchance" is no longer admissible. Experimental work on sleep monitoring and Rapid Eye Movements (REM) (Fisher, 1965) demonstrates that dreaming is a neurophysiological necessity and dream deprivation has serious mental and physical consequences. REM findings indicate that dreaming occurs regularly during sleep. The neurophysiological changes which take place during REM periods suggest that activation of the limbic area of the brain—an area associated with primitive functioning of drives and affects—is involved. Such neurophysiological retrogression supports Freud's theory of the dream as a regressive phenomenon which returns us to primitive states of infancy. While recent research in sleep monitoring has turned up significant findings on the obligatory nature of dreaming, its length and recall, this research has not yet yielded information on the dream's content or formation.

So far as we know, dreams are produced by bursts of psychic activity which, because sleep cuts off the possibility of voluntary motor action, seek sensory release. In addition to limiting physical mobility, the sleeping state reduces contact with the external world, and so the perceptive function of the ego, itself never totally asleep, has more energy to devote to internal psychic activity. When normal waking control and censorship of antisocial impulses are partially abandoned, a set of conditions favorable to the production of a dream is established.

SOURCES OF THE DREAM

Every dream owes its content to both past and present. From the remote past come infantile experiences and memories as well as drives seeking satisfaction. No dream can exist without the impetus of a wish representing the claim of an instinctual drive which, although infantile in origin, retains an appetite for gratification throughout life. As infantile drives make their way upward into the dream, months, years, or perhaps decades after their origin, they are accompanied by an apparatus of inhibitions and prohibitions, innate or acquired, and just as primitive in character. We refer to the portion of the dream that owes its derivation to the impulses, feelings, and ideas of early life as "the dream from below."

Current experiences, affects, hopes, fantasies, conflicts, and disappointments, whether conscious or unconscious, also make a contribution to the dream. We call that part of the dream produced by current stimuli "the dream from above." While it is true that dreams owe part of their content to a current mental event, the day residue is not sufficient to produce them. A dream is formed only when the current event makes contact with an impulse from the past—specifically, with an infantile wish. Sometimes a contemporary experience is so evocative of an earlier one that it pulls to the surface an infantile drive for gratification which might otherwise have remained dormant. Conversely, a remote event, by virtue of its persisting importance, may invest a recent experience with a significance it would not have had in its own right.

Inasmuch as we conceptualize the quality of mental events according to their relation to consciousness, the content of the dream belongs to qualitatively different states of consciousness as well as to different periods of life.

When we refer to dreams in a theoretical sense, we have in mind three distinct entities: manifest dream, latent dream thoughts, and dream work. What the patient recalls and relates as his dream, the manifest dream, is a cryptic message which requires deciphering. Underlying the manifest dream are ideas and feelings, some of which belong to the present, some to the past, some of which are preconscious, some unconscious: the latent content. Interested though we are in the manifest dream, we are even more interested in the latent thoughts which give rise to it. We are equally concerned with the method whereby these latent thoughts are transformed into the images recalled as the dream. The process responsible for this alteration, which Freud considered the essential part of dreaming, is called the dream work.

Dream Work

The most arresting feature of the manifest dream lies in its apparent indifference to rationality, logic, and coherence. Gender is no longer absolute, physical assault and violence become indistinguishable from erotic passion, pleasure merges with pain, attraction with revulsion, horror with fascination, and condemnation with approval. Although the dream appears quite mad, there is method in it.

When we regress during sleep, we do so not only in a temporal sense, but in a functional one. The regression is partially to a primitive, archaic mode of mental operation typical of earliest mental activity, i.e., to primary-process functioning. Primary process, characterized by diffuse, random, and uncontrolled discharge of excitation, presses for immediate release and tolerates not the slightest delay. Jumping as it does from one idea or image to another with complete disregard for rational considerations, it more closely resembles a flow of energy than thinking. The dream work operates according to the principles governing primary process, and this, for the greatest part, explains the bizarre quality of the manifest dream. The mobility of psychic energy in the primary process and its inexorable demand for immediate discharge account for the mechanisms of condensation and displacement employed by the dream work.

Condensation

Condensation, the fusion of two or more ideas or mental images, created the centaur, mermaid, sphinx, and the host of composite creatures found throughout mythology. It also produces the composite figure found in the dream. At its simplest, such a figure combines one or more features of one person with those of another.

> My mother was speaking, but not with her own voice. It sounded just like my sister. And she had the red hair of my other sister, and she was wearing one of her dresses.

The dreamer made clear in her associations that she could sum up all she felt about her mother by putting together those of her sisters' characteristics she liked least.

We get the same effect when we telescope two words— as in Joyce's neologisms "Moansday, Tearsday, Wailsday, Thumpsday, Frightsday, Shatterday," for instance—or when we combine a word with a feeling tone as Winston Churchill did in pronouncing "Nazi" to make it sound as "nasty" as possible. As a matter of fact, neologisms are common in dreams.

Primary-process transfer of cathexis provides the impetus for sweeping up related concepts into a unity. A single representation carries multiple messages. When we undo the work of condensation through free association and restore the referents which have been joined into one, we bring to light a long chain of ideas. For example, in this dream:

> A woman teacher is seated at a desk in a classroom. She is talking Rumanian.

So far as the dreamer was concerned, the operative idea in this terse dream was the speaking of Rumanian. His mother spoke Rumanian; he loved to hear her talk in this exotic language. He wanted his analyst to talk to him so he could soak up the words and feel nourished. In his fantasies, psychoanalysis was a feeding and Rumanian a secret language of love. Without associations to Rumanian, we should never have expected to find condensed into this brief dream a veritable saga of love—of childhood love for his mother. The dream element, "talking Rumanian," amalgamated all this in a single stroke.

The dream work's capacity for condensation is enormous. Analysis must reconstitute the distillate. In waking moments, we have far less to say than we care to acknowledge; in our dreams we convey far more than we imagine. A man dreamed:

> I stood at the door of a classroom. Nobody was in the room except a teacher who pointed to a bookcase which contained copies of *The Book of Knowledge* in Latin. I was surprised because I'd never heard of a Latin edition.

At least five determinants for the image of the "teacher" in the dream were uncovered. The teacher in question was stern but kind; so was the dreamer's father (Latin was the language of a people who imposed law and order). The real teacher had died in an automobile accident. At the time of the dream, the patient was preoccupied with thoughts of death. The real teacher had been German. The dreamer had an abiding hatred for Germans. The dream teacher was masculine. The dreamer was involved in an affair with a teacher and was afraid she might be pregnant. Always uneasy with women, he turned to men for companionship. Men were a protection against women. And so the dream statement "teacher" does duty for a wide variety of memories and preoccupations.

> An automobile in a garage with all its machinery out on a workbench, its convertible top half-raised.

This brief dream elicited the following associations. The dreamer was in analysis and felt stripped, as if his insides were exposed ("out on a workbench"). He worried about potency and erection ("half-raised top"). His father was an auto buff, adept at mechanics, and frequently called for the patient's assistance. The patient had masturbated in the garage. He loved the garage because he played there, hated it because having to help his father interfered with his fun.

Condensation effects a tremendous economy in time and energy. The saving in expenditure produces pleasure, as illustrated by the patient who, knowing his analyst drove a Humber, reported this dream:

> I was driving around and around the block where your office is. Suddenly I realized that the car I was driving was a Singer. I began to laugh and couldn't stop. I woke up laughing.

It was left for the analyst to explain just why the patient was laughing.

Displacement

Like condensation, displacement, the second essential mode of dream-work operation, is the result of the rapid transfer of energy from one idea or image to another, characteristic of primary process. The two mechanisms are intimately related and share responsibility for a major part of dream distortion. Whereas condensation distorts the latent thoughts by fusing or telescoping, displacement acts by a shift of emphasis or value. Displacement assumes myriad forms; the transposition can involve people, places, objects, actions, or affects. A woman troubled by intense competitiveness with her brother for their parents' love dreamed:

> I was standing in a very definite place in a very definite house. It was the house we lived in when my brother was born. I stood in what had been my play area. I saw a ball lying in front of me and gave it a hard kick.

She had talked, the day before, to a man who resembled her brother, and had arrived home feeling unaccountably irritable. Without any provocation from her husband, she criticized him scathingly and then retired to bed, in tears. The husband at home and the ball in the dream suffered what was intended for her brother.

A patient had this dream after saying he wanted to break off psychoanalysis but was afraid of the consequences.

I went into the drugstore on the corner near your office. The place seemed to be doing badly and on the point of closing. Behind the counter, a clerk dreamed away. He paid no attention to me and I thought, "This won't last long."

The dreaming clerk replaced the analyst who "won't last long." The drugstore bore a faint therapeutic resemblance to the analyst's office. Displacement involved both locale and people.

Here is a dream illustrating a double displacement.

I am with my sister-in-law watching a girl in a movie. She is nude except for a fishnet covering, and she dances sensuously. I become the girl and then a cat. The cat corners me in a room and won't let go.

The dream displaced the woman's sexual frustration onto a dancing girl and then to the cat. A further displacement occurred in the substitution of the movie for analysis.

Besides transposing objects, people, and places, displacement creates further ambiguity by offering a part for the whole. A woman had this dream:

I was looking in a shop window at a display of lingerie. There were silk stockings draped attractively as only the French can arrange them. In one corner was a model of a leg with an unusual piece of hosiery. It stood out, and I stared at it for a long time. It reminded me of something but I couldn't say what, or why it was so fascinating.

17

Her fantasies concerned breasts and genitalia, but her dream referred only to the leg. The leg substituted for a penis, which in turn substituted for the whole person. Genitalia are frequently displaced upward as well as to other areas of the body.

The following dream illustrates the close relationship between displacement and condensation.

I seemed to be in the neighborhood of the house where I was born. There was a light in the window.

The casually seen house and light were connected with the patient's grief over his father's death. Neither the event nor his reaction was contained in the dream's indifferent content. Such omission is characteristic of displacement in the dream. The dream-work mechanisms have shorn the event of its emotional intensity.

A variant of displacement results in reversal, a particularly effective means of distortion. The dream speaks of crowds when it in fact refers to something secret; it multiplies parts of the anatomy as an allusion to the absence of such parts; it assigns, as in this case, the dreamer's intentions to another person:

I was lying on a couch when someone behind me reached over and banged me on the head.

The patient's observable hostility and resentment made clear exactly who wanted to do the banging.

The dream work reverses not only the direction of an action and the roles within it, but also turns affects completely around.

In the street. Nobody was there, but I felt shame and embarrassment which then turned into terror. I thought there were a million eyes on me.

The dreamer was preoccupied with fantasies of prostitution and exhibitionism. The dream replaced the positive pleasure provided by her sexual fantasies with the negative affects of shame and terror. The arena of her fantasies was heavily populated; the dream street was emphatically empty.

A young man who had gone to extraordinary lengths to avoid being drafted dreamed:

I was in a large board-room with a lot of people sitting around. I had taken a test. I had a sheet of white paper in my hand. I had failed the test and was ashamed in front of all those people. But nobody took the slightest notice of me. Nobody paid any attention.

Here the shame is not the subject of reversal, but reflects the man's attitude toward what he saw as his own reprehensible behavior. "Nobody paid any attention" is the opposite of his fear that everyone will know what he has been doing. This dream can be placed in that group of classic dreams of nudity accompanied by a remarkable indifference on the spectators' part to the dreamer's condition. The dream spectators are every bit as hypocritical as the naked emperor's cheering subjects. They know perfectly well what is going on, but expediency demands that they too close their minds to it. And whoever else the dream spectators may represent, they also stand for the dreamer himself. As a matter of fact, anybody of either sex will serve as stand-in for the dreamer so long as a basis for comparison exists between them.

> Clark Gable was on the street crying. He looked sick. I tried to help him.

Here the actor's large ears served as the connecting link. The dreamer's fantasies of world fame and success with women contributed to Gable's presence in the dream.

The following fragment shows the operation of both condensation and displacement. It was presented during a period of positive transference, the day after a patient had curbed her impulse to masturbate.

> I was in a house high up on a hill or in the air. I could look out over a jocular view. Even in the dream I thought this a funny way to conceive of it.

Her dream conveyed an air of pleasure and good will. Sexual undertones were conspicuous. "Jocular" made her think of "jockey shorts" and "jock straps." The "view" was a condensation of her pleasure in looking and of having taken a reflective look at her sexual behavior. The wish to view the male genitals was transferred to the harmless aerial view of a landscape. A "funny" conception was a witty replacement for her interest in the male genital which she simultaneously admired and derided. At the same time, she asserted herself by taking a lofty "view" and making a joke of her wish.

An inordinately narcissistic man, who made a career of exploiting women and discarding them, was confronted by a particularly tenacious lady who, for reasons of her own, wanted him to marry her. For equally compelling reasons, he was resolved to withstand the siege. In one of his dreams, a single underlying theme was displaced successively, in layers as it were, from top to bottom.

> I was having my analytic session. I kept repeating, "I don't want to get married, I don't want to get married." I left and went down to find my car. It was nowhere to be seen. I looked everywhere but couldn't find it. Then I saw a ravishing girl walking away from me. I felt compelled to follow her. Next I was in my apartment on my knees examining my rug. I wanted to change it so I had cut a swatch from it to use. I called to a girl who was in the room and at the same time in a distant city to help me shop for a new rug. Then two men put their arms around me and wanted to kiss me.

"No marriage" first appears directly in speech, then as the loss of his car (symbol, in this instance, for a woman), again as following another girl. It next declares itself as changing his rug (again a symbol for a woman) and calling on a girl who is both there and not there. Finally, the dream reflected the deepest layer of his aversion to marriage by its reference to homosexuality.

Symbols

The dream-work mechanisms of condensation and displacement are supplemented by symbolization, which further obscures the latent thoughts. Symbolism is a universal primal language representing an association between ideas having something in common although the relationship is not always easily discernible. Symbols stand for primary ideas from which they acquire their significance. The association is made not by the reasonable adult mind, but by the infantile unconscious one which typically equates objects that appear to have something in common. For a child, whose interests are always specific and physical, the concrete automatically takes precedence over the abstract. Symbolic language employs an elementary means of conceptual identification inherent in the child but, aside from psychotics and certain artists, strange to adults. Failure to recognize the connection between the symbol and what it stands for stems from man's having forgotten the infantile ways of thinking of which the symbol is a persistent remnant. Temporal regression, so inevitable a characteristic of sleep and dreaming, brings in its train perceptual and conceptual regression which leads to the formation and use of symbols.

Throughout recorded history, symbolism used in literature, art, religion, folklore, and mythology as well as in everyday life has found acceptance as a means of communication. Curiously, the application of symbolism to dream interpretation is often regarded as arbitrary and generates suspicion, suggesting that an irrational influence is responsible for its rejection in this area.

Each dreamer employs a preferred set of symbols chosen from the vast number available to him and uses them with considerable regularity and consistency so that they become a sort of mental fingerprint.[1]

The experienced analyst can sometimes make an im-

---

[1] A recurrent use of the same symbol must have a special significance but, to date, in not a single instance have I been able to trace any to its source in the patient's personal experience. Why does anybody use a particular symbol with such consistency that one could call it a mannerism?

mediate translation of the manifest content on the basis of typical symbolic images in the dream. The interpretation of symbols without an intimate knowledge of the dreamer, however, without conceding any relevance to his current circumstances, may be intellectually stimulating but is not a valid exercise in a properly conducted analysis. Even though an invariant symbol may be present, only an appraisal of each dream on the basis of all the dreamer's associations can produce an accurate reading. Very occasionally, the symbol may stand solely for itself. We cannot isolate symbols from the rest of the dream or the patient.

Referents for symbols are surprisingly limited in number. They correspond to the basic and universal preoccupations of children: birth, death, the body and its functions, the sexual organs, and people, especially members of the family. The wide discrepancy between the profusion of symbols and the ideas symbolized (for all their basic biological identity, we would not expect the Australian bushman to express himself in the language and style of an Oxford don) inevitably evokes a reaction much like the one that led Freud (1916, p. 154) to observe, ". . . in contrast to the multiplicity of the representations in the dream, the interpretations of the symbols are very monotonous, and this displeases everyone who hears of it; but what is there we can do about it?"

The student of the dream must be well acquainted with the symbols he will meet. In a compassionate effort to spare him the tedium of an exhaustive listing, I offer the most commonly encountered. The illustrative material on the clinical use of the dream will contain still others.

Man's interest in and preoccupation with the way he

enters and leaves the world is reflected in the large number of symbols for birth and death. Water, primarily immersion in it, always refers to pregnancy and birth. At the same time, water or anything flowing has important oral connotations and is intimately connected with urinary fantasies and experiences. Infestation with vermin or insects refers to semen and impregnation. Sleep, silence, descending into the earth, dwindling in size, taking a trip (especially westward), disappearing into a blanket of fog may all appear as symbolic variants of death.

The Greeks used the configuration of the human body as the basis for their architecture. In the dream, human anatomy is symbolized by buildings, with windows and doors corresponding to the body orifices. Symbolization borrows heavily from nature to represent anatomical parts and zones: landscapes, mountains, valleys, forests, and flowering gardens frequently appear. Caves instantly convey the idea of body cavities; ledges and overhangs, whether architectural or natural, usually portray breasts, as do sisters or fruit. All articles that enclose space or are capable of being entered qualify as symbolic representatives of the female genitalia. The horseshoe renders their shape, jewels their value; shellfish and the mouth almost speak for themselves. Stoves, closets, and cupboards refer more to the uterus than to the vagina. Undergrowth and underclothes are genitalia in general. Stairways, ladders, corridors, and tunnels often appear in dreams referring to the female genitalia; when a red lining is added, the meaning becomes unmistakable. The street, too, is a sexual symbol—the place for traffic with women. A patient dreamed of standing on a street watching a procession of wagons go by. The wagons contained barrels with the number "zero" painted on them.

This man was beset by the problem of compulsive promiscuity and was unable to rid his mind of the thought of bedding every woman he encountered on the street. He recalled his dream after reading *The Story of O.*

Lewin (1948a) has called attention to the meaning of "nothing" as signifying the vagina. A married lady introduced almost every analytic session with "I have nothing to talk about," before going on to the news of the day, which usually consisted of disparagement of men—her husband in particular—and her feeling that she could do better without them.[2]

Allusions to the color red may represent menstruation, which is also symbolized, I have found, by "falling off," an expression sometimes used by girls to refer to it. A lady expecting her period dreamed she climbed a building, peered over the edge of the roof, and was afraid she would fall off. Whether or not it is correct to call this a symbol is arguable. It is sometimes hard to draw the line between symbolism and other means of representation.

Flowers, like eyes, can stand for either male or female genitalia. So does the ship which, in the one case may be represented as cleaving through water, and in the other as a vessel.

The phallus is symbolized by anything resembling it in form, function, or general properties as, for example, the bridge which joins two bodies. All penetrating, expandable, collapsible objects serve as symbols for the penis. Elevators, airplanes, birds or projectiles, things which go up and down may be symbolically employed for the male organ as may cameras and instruments which can be manipulated or

---

[2]Cf. dream, "President gives her a fountain pen" (p. 183).

played upon. The man who dreamed of an automobile with its parts out on a workbench and its convertible top half raised[3] was preoccupied with his potency. A more recondite equivalent is the number three which has been found, apart from the dream, in widely separated parts of the world in the form of the triskelion, the fleur-de-lis, and the tripod.

A constant symbolic association exists between the phallus and animals, from the rat to the elephant. The snake and serpent are age-old and tediously familiar. By extension, we see why lengths of rope or hose are gross phallic equivalents. A woman whose penis envy made a significant contribution to her character disorder dreamed:

> ... a little boy holding a fox in his hands. It was a tiny, perky, red-nosed animal, more like a toy, but it could bite. Suddenly it appeared from out of his pocket, withdrew and emerged from his fly.

The little man as portrayed by the dwarf, anything mysterious and having to do with conjuring, such as amulets or charms, even the devil himself, appear in dreams as substitutes for the penis. Articles of male attire, especially cloaks and neckties, are common phallic symbols. The same is true of the head and the hat; hence beheading is feared as castration. A fairly common dream (I have so far found it only among women) is of having a baby that walks and talks at birth. This baby must be regarded as a substitute for the miraculous penis.

The sun is a phallic symbol, the flame invariably so. The hearth is a female symbol at which the masculine flame is kindled. Phallicism has far-reaching associations with heat

[3] See dream, "Convertible car disassembled in garage" (p. 15).

and anything else commonly identified with passion. A patient had this dream when resisting a positive transference because of its homosexual implications:

> I am sitting with my wife in an auditorium. A man is lecturing on hypnosis. The air is suddenly suffused with a strange pinkish-red glow. The hypnotist is looking at me, and I am forced against my will, pulled through the air toward him. I struggle against it, cry out, and wake up as from a nightmare.

Sometimes a body part, a protruding arm, leg, or nose, or the tail of an animal stands for the penis. This equation is universal and accounts for symptoms that would be medically meaningless were symbolism rejected. Indeed, the compendium could be continued interminably. The number of things reconstituted in the image of man's narcissism with regard to the phallus and endowed with its attributes is truly awesome.

Dreams about teeth are peculiar in that there is such a wide divergence, from any rational point of view, between teeth and eroticism. Such dreams have many variations. The teeth may be weirdly distributed in the mouth, they may be pulled out in quantities, be seen falling out of their own accord, or encountered with amazement in a newborn infant. Without exception, when teeth appear in the manifest dream as a symbol, they refer to sexuality (often with aggressive connotations) in its latent content. The reference is to masturbation, intercourse, and, in women, to unconscious fantasies of pregnancy. Loss of teeth symbolizes the loss of the penis and fear of impotence. The dream marked by loss of several teeth accentuates the fear of castration. The night after masturbating, a man whose castration anxiety was of central importance in analysis had this dream:

> I was playing ball with my father who then turned into a friend of mine. We threw the ball back and forth, harder and harder. Suddenly my friend's face grew red and swollen and he threw the ball at me with lightning speed. It hit me in the face and knocked out three teeth.

Another man sat in a taxi between two girls he was escorting home and toyed with the idea of seducing them. While preparing for bed, his fantasies led him to thoughts of masturbation. He abandoned this notion too and then dreamed:

> I was lying in bed when I remembered I had an appointment with my dentist. Then I realized I had already kept it. He had drilled a hole in two teeth, one upper left, one lower right. The holes were meant to remain holes and not to be filled.

Displacement may occasionally be made to the nose. A man resisting the urge to masturbate because he was afraid that if once he started he would not be able to stop had this dream:

> I started to pull a hair out of my nose. I was alarmed to see a whole shower of hairs come out.

Rhythmical activities from dancing to athletic games symbolize the sexual act, as do ascent or descent, entering or disappearing, waxing or waning. Dreams of flying can symbolize erection. Sexual lust with gluttonous overtones is often conveyed by dreams of banquets or heaping profusions of sweets.

Autoerotic pleasure is represented by all sorts of activity, playful and otherwise, including passive forms of motion such as being carried, pushed, or tossed about. A masturbation fantasy is symbolically expressed in this typical dream of sexual excitement:

> I entered an elevator. I felt short of breath and began to breathe more and more heavily. The elevator started up, steadily gaining speed. It reached the roof, kept on going, and shot right up and out into the air.

Symbols also appear in connection with other basic body functions. Yellow liquids have the virtue of being obvious. Symbolism in the dream equates feces with money and associates both with the idea of a gift. Excrement, referred to by the colors brown or gold, usually has a bivalent meaning; it is both worthless and of great value. The symbolic equation between feces, penis, and baby appears in symptom formation as well as in dreams.

Following a siege of constipation, a man gave himself an enema, after which he was stimulated to have intercourse. That night he dreamed:

> I came across an enormous pile of gold coins. Endless. I scooped them up feverishly. They seemed to be everywhere.

Eminent personages running the gamut from gods and royalty to senators can be used as symbolic stand-ins for parents. The ogre and devouring witch, in addition to serving as projections of oral drives, have similar symbolic significance. A room or a house may stand for a woman, a series of rooms for a series of women. Cats are common symbols for women. The mother is represented by queens, witches, or spiders. Women are also represented by a host of symbols having to do with *mater*ial: paper, wood, cloth, and objects made from them. The automobile does duty for both men and women. Animals symbolize people in general and parents in particular. Children appear as vermin, insects, or very small animals.

A man who was beginning to view his wife in a fresh and less favorable light dreamed:

> I looked at a rug on the floor of my own bedroom. It seemed changed, enlarged and ugly at one end, and out of shape. I told this to a friend who said he could always get me another rug. [4]

A patient was ashamed to tell me he had again acted out his compulsive promiscuity, but gave himself away by bringing this dream:

> I was in a bakery, a dull drab affair. I bought the best cake they had. Then I saw a lemon-iced chocolate cake. I couldn't resist. I sneaked a little piece of it, not wanting the baker to see me or charge me. I left the rest there and ran out.

If we substitute analysis for "dull drab ... bakery" and tart for the "cake," the meaning is clear enough. The "lemon-iced chocolate cake" readily suggests the range of his libidinal appetites.

MEANS OF REPRESENTATION

In addition to condensation, displacement, and symbolization, the visual means of representation demanded of the

[4] See also dream, "I don't want to get married" (p. 21).

dream result in distortion of its latent content by the use of pictorial metaphors to express certain ideas. (Affects are not similarly transformed. They remain affects, as we have seen, whether or not they are replaced by opposite affects in the manifest dream, displaced, or omitted altogether.)

The dream's ingenuity in meeting a pictorial requirement is impressive and occasionally amusing. A patient, past mistress in the art of incitement to riot by passing meretricious confidences, brought this dream after she had lied to both her husband and to me:

> My cat had gone astray. I knew cats follow a string when
> it is dragged along the ground, so I got a length of string,
> went outside, and a long line of cats followed it. Then
> two elongated mice or rats joined the line.

The two mice at the end of the string formed a rebus for the husband and myself being strung along by the patient.

To express in the shape of a picture the conditions laid down by *because, therefore, but, when,* or *if,* for example, demands graphic inventiveness. Nevertheless, the relationships commonly set forth by prepositions, conjunctions, other parts of speech, or by punctuation require visual means of representation in the dream. Causal relationships, which are usually either omitted or embodied in condensation, can also be represented by a dream divided into segments of varying lengths. The order in which these segments appear may parallel the cause and effect or may be reversed. The dream may begin with the effect and end with the cause, but in all cases the longer section corresponds to the principal clause, the shorter section to the subsidiary one.

31

When a dream tries to present a relationship between two ideas or events, it places the images which stand for them in proximity to each other, substituting a spatial for a conceptual or temporal relationship. In order to indicate the idea of superiority or advantage, for instance, the dream may place two people on different physical levels. Tiny people seen at a distance indicate events that have taken place a long time ago. Again, this is the exception rather than the rule; usually the relationship is omitted or served by condensation.

Repetition of an action within a dream or duplication of a dream element can signify that the event has occurred repeatedly.

> I saw dozens of women leaning out of windows on both sides of a street, shaking their heads in unison. Then they shrieked and waved their hands menacingly. They repeated this over and over again.

The dream alluded to the patient's relations with women. Time after time he sought them out only to rebuff them or to be rebuffed. The repeated action in the dream and the multitude of women represented a succession of rejections.

To our confusion, the idea of opposites and contrasts is indicated in the dream either by a choice of one or the other or by the insertion of both, as though they were equally valid. In a third alternative, the two may be combined in one dream element. The context determines which is intended.

A counterintention, "No, I don't want to," in the latent thoughts is represented by means of inhibited movement, by the classic dreams of paralysis. We are only too familiar with "I can't," as the unmistakable equivalent of "I don't want to." An endless variety of dreams: the missed train, the lost car, the forgotten name, as well as the dream of immobility, all bespeak the same intention—to interpose a negative wish. The similarity to parapraxes is obvious.

Critical opinions appearing in the dream belong to the latent thoughts. Derision in the latent thoughts, for example, will find expression in a manifest dream whose content conveys absurdity.

> I was buying a suit at the tailor's. A woman showed me ridiculous red herringbone suits. I fooled around with her, saying, "Yes, give me dozens and dozens. I'll take this and this and this. Give me all of them."

The ridiculous red suits expressed mockery in the latent thoughts. The patient had been highly critical of my interpretations and was making a travesty of them both in actuality and in the dream. Sometimes criticism, instead of appearing in the dream, is expressed as a means of comment. Had the patient said, "I had a ridiculous dream last night," he would have conveyed his message equally well.

SECONDARY REVISION

All the elaborate measures employed to disguise the latent dream thoughts are, according to the propositions of structural theory, at the behest of the dreamer's never totally dormant ego. Censorship, which forbids unconscious impulses expression in forms they would naturally

33

assume, opposes regressive phenomena, including the dream. But while the ego, often enough spurred on by superego requirements, supplies the motive for dream distortion, it may be by no means always satisfied with the results. An impulse, albeit disguised, has come through, and the censorious ego and superego, conscious or unconscious, react with a last-ditch effort to make the result acceptable, thereby contributing still another distorting factor to the dream.

Secondary revision, using secondary-process thinking, attempts to supply the dream with consistency and coherence, to fill in the gaps, create some sort of order, and mold it into an intelligible whole. Wherever we find continuity and logic in the manifest dream, we know secondary revision is responsible.

The expression "It's only a dream" is very familiar. Sometimes the dreamer has the thought on waking; sometimes it is incorporated directly into the dream. In either case, the judgment is made by the ego, the agent of secondary revision. That portion of the dream dismissed as "only a dream" is precisely the part that is too real for comfort. The ego, by providing false reassurance, has created another dimension to the distortion.

Freud (1900) includes among the contributions of secondary revision, the carrying over of waking fantasies into the dream. Insofar as all fantasies are in themselves distortions of infantile wishes, their appearance in a dream adds to the distortion. The patient who didn't want to get married[5] brought into his dream a ready-made waking fantasy onto which he displaced his conflict. In his fantasy, he pursued

[5]See dream, "I don't want to get married" (p. 21).

to bed every attractive girl that caught his eye; in his dream, he saw a ravishing girl walking away from him and felt compelled to follow her.

STRUCTURAL THEORY

Central to psychoanalysis and to an understanding of the dream is the concept of conflict in mental life. Before the postulation of structural theory, conflict was assumed to result from the antithesis between conscious and unconscious. Further clinical experience made it clear that resistance to the emergence of unconscious material was itself unconscious. It was found that patients, free associating with the best will in the world, were unable to recover the repressed thoughts underlying the manifest dream. Another problem arose in connection with dreams having a predominantly distressing affect. Such dreams appeared to be in flat contradiction to the thesis of the wish-fulfilling nature of the dream.

The concept of a division of the mental apparatus into id, ego, and superego resolves these apparent contradictions. Structural theory proposes that conflicts between the functions of the different structures give rise to the unpleasant features of both dream and symptom and account for the phenomenon of unconscious resistance.

We now seek to understand the nature and function of anti-instinctual forces as well as infantile, instinctual drives and their derivatives. We assume that both sets of forces and the shifting balance between them are of major importance in determining the configuration of the dream. Ordinarily, in waking hours, the exercise of ego functions is sufficient to maintain a working balance. But at night, when sleep weakens the ego functions and cuts off the external helping hand, instinct has an opportunity to reassert itself.

In our assessment of the dream, the concepts of structural theory offer additional aid. The strict independence of the systems id, ego, and superego is an illusion. Clear-cut structural distinctions are arbitrary, borne out neither in life nor in clinical experience. The structural systems are not air-tight, nor are they totally in opposition to each other. While they contend, they also cooperate on a continuum to ensure survival. Moreover, the high-level theory embodied in structural propositions, while a valuable and essential instrument for the analyst, need not reduce human motivation and behavior to quasi-mechanistic functions with discrete areas of operation.

Structural theory conceives of the id as a repository of sexual and aggressive drives from all stages of development. These drives find mental representation as wishes and fantasies which seize on the dream as an outlet for immediate satisfaction. Even in the dream, they meet with counterdemands from ego and superego.

The ego functions of integration and synthesis operate to maintain logic and order in the dream. The perceiving function of the ego also makes a contribution. The ego's mechanisms of defense and its development of anxiety oppose id-derived impulses and modify their expression. Ego functions, however, are not perpetually or by nature essentially hostile to drives. The organization of the ego exists to procure instinctual satisfaction as well.

The superego exhibits its effect on the dream by introducing guilt, remorse, and punishment for the attempt to gratify a forbidden infantile wish. As an extension of the ego, it also contributes to the creation of anxiety. Superego influence in the dream is felt as approval as well as condemnation.

No dream is ever solely an "id dream." If we employ such a term it is only to indicate that infantile wishes, the mental representatives of instinctual drives or their affects, are so strong they have gained access to the dream with less distortion than usual. Dreams from below, dominated by impulses, feelings, and ideas of early life, contain more of a contribution from the id than from any other source. From the point of view of structural theory, a preponderance of sexual or aggressive drive representations from infancy reflects the id aspects of the dream.

No dream is simply an "ego dream." This would be the designation, in terms of structural theory, of those dreams which contain a considerable amount of secondary revision, include preconscious ready-made fantasies, affects, or ideas, or introduce sensory impressions from reality and register current events—the day residue. The dream from above would fall into this category. The "ego dream" would show the effects of the ego's unconscious defense mechanisms on the expression of infantile wishes from the id.

While recent research shows that amnesia for the dream is in some measure independent of repression, and that dreams are subject to "decay," the activity of the unconscious portion of the ego largely determines whether a dream or dream segment will be recalled or forgotten. Drugs and optimal awakening time from REM sleep notwithstanding, recall and retention as well as forgetting, vagueness, and the "unreliability" of the dream are generally the work of unconscious censorship and repression from ego and superego. This explains why a device such as writing down a dream in the middle of the night or first thing in the morning is largely futile. When the unconscious is geared to thwarting the intention of analytic work, no amount of solicitation avails, but is in fact construed as importunity or censure.

No dream is ever exclusively a "superego dream." The dream of punishment, however, or the one with overwhelming feelings of guilt, unmistakably indicates the presence of the superego. Although the superego may claim an especially emphatic role in spoken words in the dream (Isakower, 1954), their appearance in the manifest content has, according to Baudry (1974), multiple meaning. Spoken words in the dream may come from what is heard, or from the verbalization of thoughts and affects. They may be derived from the id as an expression of libidinal or aggressive discharge. They may equally well be determined, for instance, by the integrative function of the ego and its requirement for coherence and logic, the product of secondary revision.

The dream not only reflects the outcome of conflict between the systems of the mental apparatus, it also demonstrates the presence of contending aims within each one of them. The dream expresses the mutual modification of opposing forces and the compromise arrived at between antagonistic strivings, e.g., between activity and passivity, between masculinity and femininity, or between communication and secrecy. It provides the meeting ground where approval and condemnation, love and hate, convenience and necessity confront and vie with each other. Every dream is a compromise formed by contributions from all three psychic structures. Id, ego, and superego, each seeks satisfaction. Just as the dream represents a compromise in this respect, so, containing as it does material from the here-and-now along with infantile wishes and experiences, it can be viewed as a compromise between past and present. The dream acts as guardian of sleep by permitting the partial gratification of unconscious wishes; it disturbs sleep to the extent of allowing these wishes any expression at all.

The difficulty and complexity of dream interpretation results from the extraordinary degree to which the latent dream thoughts are distorted in the manifest dream. To begin with, they are subject to distortion reflecting the characteristic primary-process nature of the dream work's condensation and displacement. Add to this a vast propensity for symbolization and the limitations imposed by representation largely in visual form of the ideas and feelings which go into the formation of the dream. Finally, the distortion is further exaggerated by the conflicting needs of the systems of the psychic apparatus, including the ego's need to lend logic, order, and acceptability to what it regards as illogical, disorganized, and still objectionable.

PART II

THE DREAM IN CLINICAL PRACTICE

2
Preliminary Remarks

Just as psychoanalysts use the term "interpretation" to mean both translation of the manifest dream into its latent content and communication of their findings to the patient, so they use the word "dream" in two ways. In its theoretical connotation "the dream" refers to the manifest dream, its latent content, and the dream work. In a clinical sense, however, we employ the same expression to cover not only the dream in its theoretical sense, but to include the associations it produces, the context in which it occurs, and its place in our therapeutic procedures. And so, when I refer to "the dream" in this clinical part of the book, I am employing the term as a metonymic convention. It would be more exact were I to distinguish in every case between the dream in the clinical and the theoretical sense, but it would also be very much more tedious. I mention this in order to avoid misunderstanding. I would not want to convey the impression that the claims I put forth for "the dream" are made for the dream in its narrower, theoretical meaning.

Dreams are as much as part of human life as breathing. If we are listening properly, the patient will bring us his dreams unsolicited. I have not found it necessary to remind patients that we deal with dreams; patients seem to decide this for themselves when the analytic climate is receptive, unless a deep-seated resistance has erected an impenetrable barricade to the unconscious.

The primary clinical function of the manifest dream lies in its value as a starting point for associations, which are links in a chain of indirect references, signposts pointing to the unconscious. The manifest dream "does" nothing, "means" nothing unless it serves this function. We do not permit interest in the dream to preempt consideration of the urgent problems and emotional upheavals confronting the patient. Relentless pursuit of the dream is at best the mark of inexperience, at worst a betrayal of anxiety or compulsive perfectionism. We take our most favorable position when we relax, listen, and digest. To demand more is to receive less.

We listen to the dream as we listen to everything the patient says, with *evenly divided, free-floating attention.* We endeavor to feel along with the patient. The mother feeding her child opens her mouth in unison with him; she is sharing her child's experience, just as we try to share our patient's. Indeed, an oral interchange does in fact take place between mother and child, between analyst and patient. At the same time, the mother continues to be a mother, just as we continue to be analysts. This is where the "evenly divided" enters in. Our critical faculties, though held in abeyance, continue to operate.

In principle, we listen to the dream uncommitted, neutral, without favor or criticism, and with a willing suspension of disbelief. In practice, the ideal is not always realized. The analyst's own ego state may be in a condition unfavorable to receptivity, he may have unconscious reactions to a patient's problems, may find a patient's neurosis particularly distasteful. To the extent that the analyst's personal problems and involvement generate unconscious prejudices, they interfere with his really hearing what the patient has to say. Central to the concept of analytic listening is the analyst's ability to permit his unconscious and preconscious to work for him in pursuit of the patient's unconscious. While theory is fundamental, the analyst does the patient a disservice if he allows himself to be unduly influenced by theoretical preconceptions, if he tries to force the dream to conform to them. Unless he accepts the dream on the dreamer's terms, the analyst runs the danger of doing the dream violence. If he endows a dream with his own conceits, he bars himself entry into the dreamer's world. He remembers that the dream belongs to its creator, that it offers the analyst an opportunity of listening in on a dialogue the dreamer is holding with himself.

We listen with equal care to the apparently artless asides and passing comments that attend the report of a dream. A patient's attitude to his dream reveals basic elements of character structure, tells us a good deal about the nature of his defenses, gives us clues to underlying pathology, and has prognostic significance. A man who frequently had a "fragment of a dream" to tell me showed similar reluctance to delivering anything else whole. His life was divided into compartments separating sex from love, thought from speech. Nothing came together in unity or cohesion. A woman who had a "smattering of dreams" never finished what she began, darted from one activity to another, leaving behind, like so many droppings, a trail of uncompleted projects, one of which was analysis. Another patient prejudged his dreams, prefaced literally all of them with, "I can't make anything out of it; the usual kind of dream that doesn't mean anything to me," and stripped all his other actions and relationships of meaning.

Having listened to the dream, we require associations. How do we get them? Should we ask for them directly? Should we ask for associations to each discrete element in the dream? To its most intense part or parts? To spoken words, if any, in the dream? Should we inquire about the events of the previous day?

I cannot advise a consistent, uniform approach or lay down fast rules. Circumstances and analysts' styles do differ. I am personally inclined to ask the patient, in a very general way, for help with the dream. I may or may not ask if he has any ideas about a particular part. It depends on the state of resistance, transference, therapeutic alliance, and what seems to be uppermost in his mind. For the same reasons, I may or may not ask what happened the day before or why he had the dream when he did.

What do we do when the patient has no associations to the dream and when neither context, symbols, nor knowledge of the patient are of any help? Countless times we have no choice but to let the dream drop and wait for better days. I have gone for days, weeks, sometimes even months, without being able to "do" anything with a patient's dreams. Either he had no associations or those he had left me completely in the dark.

Let us assume we know what a dream means, a large assumption indeed. How do we use our information?

Should we offer an interpretation or not? If we offer one, how do we know what to say or when to say it? Our analytic goal is to tell the patient something about himself he has not known before. Our specific technical procedure is interpretation, complete or incomplete, dynamic or genetic. Other kinds of interventions: confrontations which demonstrate connections, clarifications which contrast behavior or fantasy with reality, and reconstructions which assume the existence of a past event, are subsidiary to interpretation; they prepare the way for it and are used with this in mind.

As a compromise formation, the dream contains the claims of drive and defense, past and present, preconscious and unconscious functioning. We are consequently offered not one but several possible levels of interpretation. Faced with an embarrassment of riches, we are forced to make a selection. We might even choose to say nothing. We may have learned something, but must ask ourselves whether this knowledge will be helpful to the patient. Before saying anything, we want to be sure the patient is prepared to receive it. Patients in a state of severe resistance will hardly be open to observations tending to raise further resistance. Dreams reported by patients in acute anxiety or distress may contain useful information which, for the moment, is more valuable to us than to them. We carefully assess the state of the transference, the therapeutic alliance, and consider whether we have a reliable ego capable of absorbing what we have to offer. We also have to think of the time at our disposal. I try to avoid interpreting a dream too near the end of a session.

The very process of weighing these factors may direct us to an interpretation of resistance, transference, or anxiety.

47

Or the associations may guide us. Unsolicited, the patient may speak to a specific element of the dream or to what we privately recognize as its equivalent.

Associations are not uniformly revealing; they require constant evaluation. Some conduct us almost directly to the latent thoughts. Some are intermediate steps in the chain of causality. Others not only display little discernible relevance to the dream, but may indeed be designed to draw attention away from its latent content. Under the influence of resistance, associations may well lead us down the garden path. Psychic determinism nevertheless insures that all associations, even those which are forced or intellectualized, have value.

Lacking associations, we have to make do with only part of "the dream." In a way, what we already know about a patient constitutes a set of associations, although it is never a true substitute for them. Occasionally, we can see the relevance of a dream to an immediate event in the patient's life, even if he cannot, and we can interpret the dream from above, relating it to the day residue. We can encourage associations by calling attention to an element in the dream or by asking for additional information. Sometimes we ask the patient to tell us the dream again, but such a procedure must be used judiciously; we do not want the patient to think the dream has some sort of magical value.

Because associations to symbols are not ordinarily forthcoming, we must interpret them from our knowledge of dream symbolism. This does not, however, give us license to interpret a symbol to the patient without considering resistance, transference, anxiety, the therapeutic alliance, and the presence of a receptive ego. When we do get associations to symbols, more often than not they represent intellectual comments based on exposure to analytic jargon. There are, of course, other reasons why patients fail to associate to everything in a dream. Repression and resistance may be responsible, or absorption in one aspect of the dream, together with limitations of time, may leave no opportunity for pursuing other elements to their conclusion.

In wording our interventions, it is wise to employ a venerable educational principle and proceed from the familiar to the unfamiliar, from the known to the unknown. Equally important is knowing how much to say. Just as in this book I have refrained from burdening the dream examples with elaborate case histories in order to avoid confusion, so the analyst must beware of offering interpretations which his patients will find too involved to digest. Concrete, modest interpretations, using the language of the dream when possible, are most likely to be assimilated. It is better to let a little go a long way, to allow room for the patient to fill in for himself. Respect for the patient demands that we leave something to his imagination, that our interventions invite collaboration without precluding further joint investigation. We do not ask him to shoulder the entire burden. By giving him just enough so that he can help himself, our interventions are more effective. If we make too many connections, the patient is less apt to make them for himself. If we intervene too much, we run the risk of breaking the chain of associations and causing him to dry up. If every dream has multiple determinants, so every interpretation, if sufficiently open-ended, can have multiple appeal. Interpretations are approximations, not infallible last words.

Only rarely can we evaluate conclusively the effect of interventions by the patient's immediate response. Only too often his aim is to please or perhaps to displease. Yet even an intellectual appreciation can sometimes ripen into deeper understanding. In analysis, nothing happens precipitately or magically; the cumulative effect is what counts.

After this attempt to establish guidelines for placing the dream in clinical perspective, I have to confess that I cannot in truth always say why I intervene as I do. Retrospective examination of a session, necessary in writing this book, leads me to think that interventions are usually based on a preconscious response to a total situation.

We cannot expect to feel our way into the dream, to "get it," all at once. The student should not be discouraged when the dream eludes him. It can do the same to the most seasoned expert.

I do not find discussion of technical procedures in the abstract very rewarding and therefore limit my general remarks to the foregoing. If, after reading one of the examples in the sections that follow, you find yourself thinking, "I don't see how Altman got there," I suggest you go back and reread the material. Very often a key word or phrase that may have eluded you on your first reading will make all the difference.

3
Initial Dreams

An analysis is not necessarily "such stuff as dreams are made on," nor founded on a dream. Yet sometimes patients start treatment with the report of a dream, occasionally even because of dreams. Does the analyst then begin with the interpretation of the first dream? How can he? What if the first dream or dreams contain, as has been said, the nucleus of the neurosis or a portent of things to come? How should he know? Ignorance hampers any far-reaching understanding of a dream presented at the beginning of analysis. Whether or not we possess a biographical sketch of the patient or a conventional medical history, we know nothing about the unconscious sources from which his dream issues. If a dream brought at the start contains information relevant to the patient's most intimate problems, those perhaps at the heart of his neurosis, we can make no assumptions, no matter how experienced or clever we are, concerning its deepest significance. Nor, on the supposition that we could, would we communicate our knowledge to the patient. A venture into analysis engenders anxiety and the defenses anxiety sets in motion. Premature interpretation merely fortifies anxiety and multiplies defenses. Safeguarding the development of a therapeutic alliance constitutes our primary consideration throughout analysis and especially at its start.

Nevertheless, limitations of this order do not bind the analyst to complete passivity nor do they require him to remain silent when he is offered dreams in the earliest stages of analysis. He may not be in a position to analyze the dream from below, but he *can* use it if he approaches it from above. He does know something about the patient's current concerns, foremost among which is the intensity of his reactions to undertaking treatment. These reactions range from wildest optimism to deepest apprehension and are often a combination of both (the doctor can help but he can also hurt). The dream sheds light on the patient's prevailing attitude toward analysis and the analyst.

One set of attitudes is founded on the search for miracles, the unconscious expectation that analysis will transform inadequacy into perfection, provide peace and happiness in perpetuity, and insure forever against life's evils and vexations. Fantasies of omnipotence and grandeur predispose some patients, especially passive ones, to expect the keys to the kingdom. Old scores with the past will be settled; the state of infantile bliss will be restored. Euphoric visions of a prolonged feeding are particularly prominent in oral characters.

The following dream was brought by a young man shortly after starting treatment. It revealed what he sought in analysis and hinted at what could be expected when the transference developed.

> I was in the bathtub of the house we lived in just before my brother was born. My mother came in looking so young it seemed incredible. She started to bathe me.

The dream setting reminded him of his earliest childhood when he had his mother all to himself and they shared an exquisite communion. On first meeting me, he had been startled by the similarity between my manner of speaking and hers. She had promised him the world, had catered to his every need. Starting analysis gave him a sense of exhilaration; it would be the making of him.

This was a dream to file and remember. The inevitable disappointments would be manifest soon enough. For the present, absence of anxiety and indications that a therapeutic alliance was in its delicate prestages of incubation made intervention superfluous.

Another man presented this dream early on:

> It was a circus. A funny little man in a frock coat, top hat, and walking stick was mincing and balancing himself on a tight wire. He turned into a very elegant cat. There was a lot of applause.

He spoke nostalgically of his "salad days" when his good looks and elegant clothes elicited compliments and general admiration. He had always wanted to be a gay cat, always been very much concerned with the impression he made.

I said, "You would like to know what I think of you." I deliberately refrained from spelling out my interpretation. To have gone further would have prematurely confronted him with a humiliating exposure of his narcissistic expectations. To have said in effect, "You want me to think you are wonderful and tell you so," would have been true but hardly discreet at this point, hardly conducive to establishing a good working relationship. Circumspection was all the more necessary inasmuch as the "tight wire" hinted at the tension underlying his narcissistic performance and indicated that he was making a plea for acceptance. Clearly, he was very unsure of himself and wanted reassurance. My intervention implied recognition of his cry for help.

So early in analysis so as to constitute a prologue, a young lady brought this dream:

> I was in a library in England. All the books bore German titles. Many people were speaking in German, but one spoke English. It grew dark and I felt like sleeping. The English voice said, "All right."

Owing to some idiosyncrasy in my voice or appearance, people seem to think I am English. I could therefore assume that the dream voice referred to me. German, a language intimately associated with psychoanalysis, alluded to the patient's apprehensions on starting treatment.

The patient said that as a child she had performed a bedtime ritual of asking her parents to tell her that "everything is going to be 'all right.' " "At our first meeting," I said, "when we made our arrangements for analysis, I used the words 'all right' to indicate that we could go ahead." She was astonished at the coincidence and told me that my use of that particular word had seemed enormously significant to her, crucial and uncanny.

All unwittingly, I had struck a responsive chord; the link

between past and present had been established. The patient was carrying over to me her expectations from her parents. I therefore did not make the interpretation more explicit, i.e., "You want me to reassure you just as your parents used to do." I did not wish to disturb the beginnings of the transference.

In contrast with the stars-in-the-eyes approach to starting analysis is the attitude of grim foreboding. The longer psychoanalysts are in practice, the more they are apt to forget just how frightening the uninitiated find their field. Many people regard with alarm the prospect of a visit to a physician of any kind. Psychoanalysis and its morbid associations with mental disorders are infinitely more alarming. Uppermost in many a patient's mind are misgivings concerning the step he has taken. No matter how highly recommended the doctor may have been, the patient has reservations about placing himself in the hands of a stranger. He wonders whether his condition is serious, whether he can be cured. In spite of his apparent composure, compliance, indifference, or even levity, he may well be beset by many if not all of these qualms. Nor is his apprehension without justification. The analytic situation brings him closer to his unconscious, and initial encounters with the unconscious, even brief skirmishes with it, can produce panic.

A man starting treatment dreamed:

> I was in a state hospital. Patients were standing around in strange attitudes but making no sound. It was awful. I could feel my skin crawl. Suddenly a huge insane man picked me up in one hand and held me to him as though I were a helpless child. I screamed in terror and woke up.

The patient alluded to people he knew who had been in mental hospitals. Although he said nothing about his fear of insanity, I realized that he saw analysis as a terrible threat. I wanted him to know I recognized his fear and therefore said, "You might worry that analysis will cause you to go crazy and lose control of yourself."

Many years ago a man brought this dream at the start of his analysis:

> I was outside a house in a field in the midst of a violent thunderstorm. It was horrid and frightening. I saw a light in the window of the house and under it, your face leering and grimacing menacingly at me. I shrieked and rushed to the window to strike. I woke up bathed in sweat.

He proceeded to fulminate against all doctors and against analysts in particular until I interrupted, "It must be very upsetting to come here to a stranger with your private affairs and not know what is going to happen."

I acknowledge this dream alarmed me. I was, after all, as unfamiliar with the patient as he with me. Moreover, I had been led to believe that a violent dream involving the analyst undisguised, at the beginning of analysis, was an ominous prognostic sign forecasting an ineffective therapeutic alliance, an unmanageable transference, severe acting out, or potential psychosis. I therefore proceeded with utmost caution. Three years later, the patient satisfactorily completed his analysis at the age of sixty-five. The prognostic significance attached to dreams of this nature, as Rosenbaum (1965) has pointed out, need not be inevitably poor.

A thirty-year-old man, Roy L.,[1] with a history of a long-standing hysterical and depressive character disorder, presented this dream in the first week of his analysis:

> I saw a soldier lying supine on a stretcher. It was being carried by four soldiers, one at each corner. I saw that where his penis should have been was a healed scar. I knew "it had happened" a long time ago.

After a brief pause, Roy L. said, "The man lying on that stretcher reminds me of myself on this couch. The scar makes me think of one I saw on a boy a long time ago. He'd had a mastoid operation and the scar really frightened me. I was afraid to ask why or how he had gotten it. I was terrified the same thing would happen to me and kept asking my parents for reassurance."

The dream warned me to proceed with due regard for his conception of analysis as invasion, as mutilation. It amalgamated levels of anxiety reaching far back to fear of death and castration, but the immediate relevance of these precursors was to the beginning of analysis and what it meant to him. I therefore made a reconstruction upward, "You are worried that analysis will take something away from you."

Roy, because of repression, did not know that the early memory was related to the current situation. Had I attempted to make the connection for him at this time, he would have been unprepared to receive or digest it. We shall meet Roy L. again in our section on anxiety. Meanwhile, we see how pathology which became manifest only later on was already adumbrated in this early dream.

---

[1] Of course, I do not address patients by their first names. I have given fictitious names to those patients whose dreams appear throughout the book. My use of first names is merely a literary device to help the reader distinguish one patient from another.

In ten consultations spread over a period of eight weeks, a man, a virgin at thirty-two, let me know he asked no favors, allowed no intimacies; that *noli me tangere* was his watchword, "I'll do it myself," his governing passion. In his childhood, his parents had taken him to a psychiatrist because of intractability both at home and in school. During his twenties, he terminated two brief courses of psychiatric treatment in the belief that he could handle his problems himself. Depression and "dissatisfaction with the way my life is going," together with several recent outbursts of uncontrollable rage, left him less certain that he could still do so. During the eight weeks I saw him face to face, he brought me no dreams. The day after his first analytic session, he reported this one, saying it had disturbed him:

> X was pregnant. She was married but she might leave her husband. If I waited for her she might become available to me. I kissed her on the forehead.

After saying that X was the girl he knew who had been talking of getting married, and that he had just told his pregnant cousin that he was starting analysis, he launched into a pedantic rendition of his history of sadistic fantasies, nosebleeds, insomnia, his masturbation and the guilt it produced—he had masturbated last night.

"Last night?" I asked, in an attempt to explore a possible connection between masturbation and the dream. As if I had not spoken, he went on to wonder if he could share anything with a woman, and expressed a preference for being by himself. Finally, he mentioned having felt upset by the change in treatment.

"Upset?" I asked, to keep him to the present.

"Well, yesterday as you got up you looked tall and imposing. I thought of an erect penis."

He returned to the dream. The sentimentality in it disturbed him. He always loathed sentiment, did not want to get involved with girls, preferred to masturbate and live in fantasies.

"You are afraid of getting involved here," I said, in recognition of his resistance.

"Oh I know it! Even as you are saying it I am getting a queasy feeling in my stomach. I don't want you to get near me. If I ever do relax, God knows what kind of impulses would come out of me. I might even have an erection here."

He devoted the rest of the session to a denigration of psychoanalysis, Freud, and myself and expressed doubts concerning his resolution to undertake psychoanalysis.

The manifest dream, read literally, is a faintly disguised rendition of the oedipal drama. Without his associations and his behavior during the hour, I would not have understood it. Taken in context, it confirms his resistance, his ambivalence to starting analysis, and more than hints at his fear of homosexuality in the developing transference. The "pregnant" girl was connected with his cousin and analysis, itself full of pregnant possibilities. "She might leave her husband"; he might leave analysis, "might" or might not be "available" for it.

My first question was obviously premature, for he apparently paid no attention. My second question was only a degree more successful as attested to by the contrived quality of his response. My third intervention, centering on resistance, evoked a very different reaction. The progression of events demonstrates that, in the interest of fostering a therapeutic alliance, attention to resistance takes first place.

At the start of his analysis, a patient reported a dream, saying it had made a profound impression on him. He was astonished to have come up with something he had certainly not thought about for thirty years.

> I was in a room of the house I lived in until I was six. I saw my old Teddy bear, one whose eyes lit up. It seemed to float in the air and then come right up to my face and look me right in the eye. I woke up.

He could remember having been very fond of the Teddy bear and of taking it to bed with him every night. He then recalled how miserable he had been when it somehow disappeared.

In the absence of further associations and with my limited knowledge of the patient, I could only surmise that the dream, with its evocation of childhood, had to do with starting analysis and possibly with his feelings about me.

Months later, when the transference had been established, I had occasion to tell the patient I noticed he had trouble meeting my eyes when I greeted him. In response, he recalled how his mother used to put her face close up to his and say, "Look me straight in the eyes and tell me the truth and I won't punish you." He had taken her at her word only to discover she hadn't meant it. After several unhappy experiences, he had learned not to trust her.

I remembered his early dream of the Teddy bear peering intently into his eyes and would have made a transference interpretation at this point had not more urgent matters prevented it. Here then were two more occasions on which

I did not "use" the dream in the sense of interpreting it to the patient. The dream nevertheless helped me to understand the nature of the transference and illuminated a life pattern I had, already observed—the patient's ambivalence with respect to trusting people, including myself. The dream had been stimulated by starting analysis and the implication of subjecting the past to review—"look me in the eye—tell me the truth." The Teddy bear, like his mother, was both friend and foe. It had betrayed him by disappearing as his mother had betrayed him by punishing him. Would the analyst betray him too? The dream contained a summary statement of his object relations, of the beginning of transference, of his intellectual curiosity based on voyeurism (the intently peering, brightly lit eyes), of grief over the loss of an infantile companion and of his childhood. All these salient experiences, hopes, and fears were telescoped in the figure of the little Teddy bear. My understanding of the dream came only in retrospect. More often than otherwise, the meaning of an early dream becomes plain only months or even years after we hear it.

4
Resistance in the Dream

The development of resistance during the course of analysis is disconcerting, disheartening, and inevitable. Having chosen to undertake an exploration of his mental and emotional life, the patient exhibits signs of aversion to the very mission he set out to accomplish. The mere prospect of exposing the unconscious sets a counteraction into motion. All the reasons for coming to analysis seem to evaporate. The interval between seeking and rejecting help may be neither decent nor discernible. Resistance may betray itself abruptly or insinuate itself gradually, but there is no staying it.

An obstacle to analytic progress and paradoxically one of its essential ingredients, resistance accompanies literally every stage of treatment. When employed in a psycho-analytic sense, resistance is not a pejorative concept. We do not conceive of it in its everyday connotation but regard it as an unconscious defense aimed at keeping the unconscious buried by obstructing the analytic process itself. We recognize it as an inveterate constituent of analysis, demanding constant consideration. We shall meet it to some extent in every dream presented here.

Resistance makes use of all parts of the psychic apparatus. The forms it assumes reveal basic components of the patient's character structure and illuminate life-long defensive ego attitudes. Patients unconsciously introduce an id factor into resistance by clinging to infantile cravings activated by regression. In analysis, we expect and even encourage regression, yet we have to remember that it can become a satisfaction in its own right. The superego, particularly as it functions archaically in opposition to all forms of gratification and well-being, supports resistance by negating therapeutic progress and maintaining self-condemnation. The contributions to resistance from all three structural systems are apparent in the dream.

If our efforts to free the unconscious from repression are to be of any avail, interpretation of resistance, like that of any defense, generally precedes analysis of drive. This applies with equal pertinence to resistance and drive as they appear in the dream. The dream with its associations helps us estimate the balance between the two forces and enables us to evaluate the ego state in which they are embodied.

Resistance introduces formidable and baffling changes into the analytic climate. The many disguises it assumes make its recognition difficult. The dream not only helps reveal its presence in anticipation of other avenues of information, but is also a means of bringing resistance to consciousness. The dream provides a sensitive approach to both the form and the unconscious infantile origins of resistance and enables us to trace out its finer structure. Later on, when I refer more explicitly to anxiety, we shall examine the role the dream plays in uncovering this source of resistance. The dream is indeed the royal road to the detection of the protean aspects of resistance.

A perpetual effort to hold the center of the stage and eclipse her older brother dominated Jenny K.'s childhood. Her parents were no match for her in energy, intelligence, or volatility; neither could meet her insatiable demands. She married before she was twenty and left her husband shortly after their child was born. She then successfully prepared herself for and entered a professional career. When a second marriage ended unhappily, Jenny, at twenty-four, bitterly disappointed that her ambitions in love and work had not been fulfilled, decided to seek help.

The following dream made plain how Jenny invested the transference with infantile yearnings, the strength and tenacity of which were potent factors in maintaining her resistance to change.

> Going up a mountain to a house. There were three roads to take. I met a man, a Negro, kind and gentle but nevertheless with a menacing quality about him. I asked him the way. Huge drifts of snow were everywhere. He advised against going up. I went anyway. Then I stood on a balcony overlooking a gorgeous view of serenity and silver clouds. It was very beautiful.

Perhaps the dream had something to do with the way she felt this morning—so wonderfully serene for a change.... The man made her think of me; my voice was so gentle and quiet, hers so raucous. She used to sparkle so, have so much more self-assurance than now. If only she could go back to

65

those times! She felt more sanguine about the future, but what if she reverted to her old ways? Only fear of my disapproval prevented her from embarking on another love affair. If she did, would she still be frigid? Suddenly she felt an ominous hardening in the pit of her stomach. She was afraid I would say something to throw a monkey wrench into her lovely mood. This serenity couldn't last, she would probably feel rotten by tonight.

Jenny's dream dealt with the pursuit of alternate courses. Contrary to the advice of a man portrayed in unmistakably ambivalent terms, she took the road leading to the restoration of infantile bliss, surrounded by the gleaming clouds of her mother's breast, where all was serene and free from conflict. The associations compared the past with the present, to the benefit of the former, and viewed the future with misgivings. Her associations gave warning that the bubble of fantasy must burst.

"It felt good," I said, "to dream of the time when you were young and carefree. Then you wake up disappointed to find it isn't true. If only you didn't have to be bothered with analysis."

"Even though I know you've helped me a lot already," she said, "I often don't want to go on. Last night I was hating you and wanted to quit and then a wave of warm love overwhelmed me."

The regression induced by analysis reactivated instinctual drive demands of earlier developmental levels with their insistence on satisfaction. In addition, the dream demonstrated how resistance makes use of the transference. Following the lead provided by the patient's associations, my intervention centered on resistance. On a deeper level, the dream figure whose advice she ignored was originally her mother. Just as fear of my criticism deterred her from pursuing her pleasures without inhibition, so at one time did her mother interfere with her gratifications. In assigning me the role of parent surrogate, Jenny's infantile claims for redress were laid at my door. My interpretation alluded to this but was adapted to her current circumstances, to the consequences of her wish to regress.

One day, during this relatively halcyon period, Jenny, who usually flashed me a radiant smile by way of greeting, entered my office glowering and announced she felt simply awful. She blamed me for not helping her; she hated everybody, was "obviously getting nowhere." She supposed I would regard her outburst as a dust storm to obscure something more fundamental, but if this were so, she had no idea what it could be. Jenny devoted the rest of the hour to bewailing her plight and lamenting my incompetence. I said nothing and consoled myself with the thought that sooner or later I would discover what was producing the storm.

The next day she greeted me cheerfully, saying she felt much better. Last night at dinner her brother had actually said something favorable about her appearance. Now she remembered a dream she had had the night before last. "When?" I asked. She had thought of telling me the dream yesterday and had decided to punish me by omitting it. But here it was:

> I was riding with my brother to a resort in the mountains. We drove up a driveway and parked before a mansion. A butler came to take my bags but another car which belonged to me stood in the way. I thought of saying, "I can move it, it's mine," but I didn't. It obstructed all passage.

She instantly connected the dream with her behavior of the previous day. After a forced literary reference to the mansion, "In my father's house are many mansions," she related the car obstructing passage to herself blocking the way in analysis, then moved on to an extended description of an incident of the day before in which she had challenged a man in her office about one of his suggestions. I interrupted her here to ask, "After the dream?"

Both the dream and her behavior bespoke resistance, but the dream gave a clue to the trend of thought generating the anxiety which underlay it. The sexual symbolism of "bags" and "riding with my brother" suggested conflict over erotic attachment to him, although without further associations the precise meaning remained obscure. The dream was the more significant for having been withheld. In this instance, resistance in the wake of anxiety contributed to the dream, to the delay in reporting it, and to the rage in the previous hour.

To ask *when* is useful in a variety of circumstances. As a preparatory intervention, it directs attention to the sequence of events and their causal relationships. The question may help restore an omission unconsciously produced in the service of resistance. It can constitute a directive to the patient for further scrutiny of events leading to and evolving from the dream. By taking *when* into account, we introduce the patient to the concept of genetic continuity, to the relationship between antecedents and consequences, to the influence of what happened before on what occurred later.

On initial interview Daniel F. impressed me as earnest and attentive but somehow just out of reach. He described his hard-working parents and his efforts to raise himself above their level socially, intellectually, and professionally. He wanted to be analyzed because he was vaguely aware that he was "missing the boat." At thirty-two, he had not yet found a girl he wanted to marry nor was he advancing quickly enough in his career to suit him. I accepted him with private reservations; there seemed to be a lack in his motivation.

It did not take long to find out what had troubled me. Daniel treated analysis as a course of instruction, with me as professor to supply explanations for him. When I failed to comply, he was not at all upset, but imperturbably went his way, listing the virtues he hoped to acquire, the defects he hoped to remedy by "disciplining himself." I saw with increasing clarity that I was dealing with an extraordinarily rigid, perfectionistic character deformation with the anal traits and stubbornness that went with it. Beyond this, he revealed little of himself. My only recourse was to steady, unremitting character analysis. It was a minor triumph when, after months of agonizing inactivity, he yielded up the following dream:

> Walking to an office. I sat down with a man on the couch. He told me to bring him a book, to go home and get it. I was suspicious. Who was he, what did he want? I saw he was wearing a police sergeant's badge and thought, "Not me. He won't get it out of me. He wants something for himself."

The couch and the room reminded him of my office. He was quite sure the dream had to do with analysis, but why the book? What was in it?. . . He was aware that he was back at procrastinating again. . . . His suspiciousness reminded him of questions he asked me and how few answers he got.... What could that book be?

"You. The bookishness you bring here to me," I said.

After mulling this over silently for some time he said, "You've often told me I speak like a book. But it's so hard for me to get anything out, so hard to be spontaneous. I wonder if you have any ideas on that."

I took advantage of the imagery in the dream to make more explicit the pedantry which constituted such an obstacle to Daniel's progress. The hour was unusual in that he not only had a dream and reported it, but his associations actually made an interpretation possible.

Hugo W. was afflicted with a character disorder which expressed itself everywhere by a rigidity so pronounced as to make contact with him virtually impossible. He rejected whatever interfered with his conception of himself as orderly and in control. For Hugo, appearances were the beginning and the end. His manners were impeccable, his attire faultless, his words and thoughts as meticulously groomed as he was. He deplored his lack of feeling, but warded off all efforts to make his posture ego-alien, clinging to his self-image as though it were necessary for survival as indeed at one time it had been.

Unfortunately, maintenance of his defensive stance demanded that Hugo blot out large segments of reality. He forgot names, events, trends of thought, and occasionally went so far as to forget what he was talking about, in which case he had to stop and build his way back to the issue at hand. He consistently forgot what took place from session to session and "free-associated" by jumping disjointedly from one subject to another. Therapeutic progress was understandably slow, the transference brittle. Several times I extended myself to break through his reserve, to evoke a response. One such attempt was made in connection with his having questioned my bill. I had to remind him I had been away for a week. The next day I asked him, with due apologies, to come at an earlier hour the following day. He replied by bringing me a dream which dramatically condensed his reaction to both my "impatience" with him and my request for a change of appointment.

> I parked my car on the street, and when I came back I found it had a green ticket. I had left it at a safe distance from a pump, but someone had pushed it in a peculiar way into the street and in front of the pump. I saw a policeman, presumably the one who had tagged me, and said to him, "My position is consistent with having been pushed." He agreed but said I would have to go to court. I asked if he would write down and sign an agreement to my position. I didn't trust him if we went to court. Then I thought, "Ah, why get involved?"

In his fragmentary way he expressed dissatisfaction with his new car, discussed litigation recently initiated by his firm, and followed this with an extended account of an argument he had just had with his wife. I interrupted to ask if he could help out a little with the dream. He described fresh examples of his forgetfulness which was becoming quite a problem, going so far as to interfere with his work. He remembered having forgotten the week I was away. He was taken aback at having to be reminded that my absence accounted for what he thought an error in his bill.

"You forget events almost as soon as they have occurred,"

I said, "especially those that take place during your analytic hour. What about that green ticket?"

"Of course, the color of your couch; we've had that before."

In the face of his palpable annoyance, I nonetheless added he also forgot I had "pushed" ahead the time for his present appointment. Silence; than more on his lack of involvement.

"My position is consistent." Indeed it was. The dream was a declarative statement: "Stop pushing me, leave me alone; I don't trust you and I refuse to get involved with you."

"You feel I should not have asked anything of you," I said.

Hugo's narcissism constituted a potent source of conscious as well as unconscious resistance in analysis, creating distrust of paralyzing proportions. He construed every attempt at contact as a humiliation and an invasion of privacy. If nothing else did, the dream made this exquisitely clear. Its coherence suggested that the ego made its contribution by introducing secondary revision in the service of resistance.

Notwithstanding the problematical influences to which he had been subjected in his early years, George G. at twenty-nine was to all outward appearance a model of propriety and diligence. The only child of a superficially sympathetic father and a domineering mother, he slept in their bedroom until he was adolescent. George listened attentively to his mother's pious maxims while he watched her lie to her friends, cheat the tradesmen, and steal removables from hotel rooms. He dutifully if unenthusiastically went away to college, but mother remained his mentor. By the time he succeeded in marrying a girl his mother by no means approved of, George's maternal identification was complete. His confusion, an inevitable consequence of his training in an atmosphere of duplicity, was pervasive. Distressed by an existence that held little direction or pleasure and alarmed at the proliferation of perverse sexual fantasies, he eventually turned to analysis for help. Here he went through the motions of eager cooperation, but it became evident that he was markedly deficient in a sense of his own identity and held few if any deeply felt convictions. While he tried hard to be candid, he could produce little more than stereotyped formulations borrowed from readings in psychoanalysis. I knew I had my work cut out for me. After one of the many occasions on which I attempted to make plain to him the difference between a genuine analytic situation and the unrealistic parental background he brought to it, he had this dream:

I was going up an elevator in a dormitory looking for a place to sleep. I couldn't find the room. I went into a bathroom and peed in a soap dish.

He felt stilted, false, unnatural.... He thought of the bathroom as a place of retreat. Right now he felt like going to the toilet. "If only you could get out of this room and pee your troubles away," I said.

He remembered an expression, "to throw or piss away the ball game." Everything he said here sounded like baloney. Whatever he did was an act. Soap reminded him of washing out somebody's mouth.

"Soft soap," I said.

"I see what you're driving at. Like a salesman, I expect

credit for what I say here. I listen to myself to see if it sounds good, if you will like it. I was thinking yesterday how I put on an act, telling you about my childhood, like a good boy."

While similar interpretations had been made before in different contexts, my intervention appeared to have made some sort of impression. George's artificiality evaporated and his subsequent remarks carried a welcome ring of truth. My interpretation was preparatory; it did not refer directly to his basic pathology, merely to one derived aspect of his unreliable ego functioning. I gave concrete expression to preconscious trends which were part of the latent content of the dream, a regressive representation of talking as urinating. If his "peeing in a soap dish" was an exhibitionistic invitation to me to admire his prowess, this was hardly the occasion for mentioning it.

The following dreams, selected from more than a dozen similar ones offered within a period of a few months, demonstrate the nature of the resistance we may expect from severely obsessional character disorders. They belonged to John Y., whose chief reason for having sought help was his distress at the remoteness which pervaded his relations with people. He had married several times, was successful enough in his career, but his professional, social, and personal life always lacked emotional purpose. So far as I could discover, his capacity for object constancy had been defective from earliest childhood. This was reflected in the transference situation, one bequeathed me by a therapist whose working arrangement with John seems never to have risen above the level of discussion. By the time these dreams appeared, he and I had had occasional sessions which went beyond this.

John dreamed frequently but dismissed his dreams as regularly as he reported them. If this was frustrating for me, it was equally so for him. He gave every conscious indication that he wanted to benefit from his dreams, but unconscious defenses minimized any advantage they might confer. After months devoted to the problem of masturbatory activities and latent homosexuality, he brought this dream:

> I was in a conference room with a man to whom I had to give a report. He looked it over and showed me it would not do. I had written on the sheet of paper sentences, about five of them, all beginning with "see." He had to cross them all out.

He supposed the dream had something to do with analysis, but aside from that, nothing occurred to him.

"No *see* here," I said, "and there were *five* sentences, just as you come here five times a week."

"That doesn't mean anything to me," John answered, a response he gave so often it had become almost automatic. He nevertheless continued with a second dream.

> General de Gaulle and I are walking up a mountain. He says nothing and neither do I. Even so, it's quite companionable and comfortable and I'm flattered. We stop for hamburgers and keep going although nothing really happens.

He reflected a bit, then granted the general reminded him of me. Nothing further occurred to him. (It occurred to *me* that he and de Gaulle shared several characteristics, including a forbidding aloofness.)

John's first dream clearly spelled out resistance to analysis; the second elaborated on the theme. Treating the two dreams as one (we expect dreams of the same night to be related), I said, "If only you could come here five times a week but not really have to say or see anything."

Another level of meaning contained in the first dream involved the operation of his superego made over to me. (The man who looked over his report said "it would not do.") The context in which the dream appeared suggested the reference was to masturbation and included a condemnation of homosexuality.

I interpreted the dreams as I did because I was sure I understood the contribution made to them by resistance, and because I knew nothing else would happen until I had dealt with that resistance.

John brought the next dream directly after he had broken off the latest in a series of very brief affairs. He had also been talking, without much conviction, of dropping treatment.

> I was traveling on a train which stopped at a station. During the wait I wandered aimlessly through the cars. Suddenly the engine started up with all the cars except the one I was prowling in, leaving me behind. I was chagrined because trains no longer spend time in stations. I had purposely let it depart without being on it, while looking around the car.

Last evening, in conversation with a girl interested in psychology, his mind started to wander and he found himself off the subject. In an effort to cover up his embarrassing lapse, he talked vaguely and ambiguously. . . . He acted here as though he weren't interested, as though analysis were an intellectual exercise. He felt toward analysis as he did toward sex; both were too much trouble and therefore to be avoided. . . . He was behaving so pointlessly it was depressing him.

"When you dismiss everything and everybody, including analysis, then you find yourself all alone, wonder why this happens to you and what will become of you," I said.

The representation of analysis by train trips is not uncommon. John's inattention (in the dream) which caused him to be left behind probably referred to his omission of the details of his sexual activity. His acting out in this arena constituted an additional dimension to his resistance.

During the weeks between the last dream and that which follows, John acted out his resistance in sexual promiscuity with a variety of women. He nonetheless continued to feel very much alone.

> I was running a long distance race all by myself. There was no one with me or anywhere around. I didn't even know what the race was about—just like here. I stopped several times at springs or wells in a cave or cavern to take a drink. I thought, "It will just be a minute and won't affect the outcome."

The dream made him think of *The Loneliness of the Long Distance Runner*, of the boy who stopped before the finish of the race at reform school just to thumb his nose in revenge at the headmaster. Of course that sounded so pat, so like his attitude toward me, it couldn't be true. (Experience with John had taught me to regard associations he qualified in this manner as having particular validity.) This past week he thought he had been seeing and learning something, but then it disappeared.

I did not intervene. I might have connected the stopping for a drink with his sexual activities, but his hostility toward me outweighed other considerations. I had to wait until conflict over acting out caused him greater distress. I was still waiting when he brought a typical resistance dream.

I had come for my appointment with the analyst. He seemed to be closeted with a company of other doctors, perhaps twenty-five of them. I was told he would have no time for me. Then I was in the waiting room. It was filled with visitors. Everyone was running around, being wild and upsetting things. An announcement was made that the doctor would not be there at all.

His use of the passive voice form and third person, the visual imagery of the manifest dream and the context in which it was produced all said, "Stay away from me." A dream containing every kind of interruption and obstacle to keeping an appointment plainly states the dreamer wants no part of analysis. In this case the dream work had reversed subject and object and displaced John's negativism onto me, while the crowd of doctors represented the latent wish to keep his sexual activities secret (crowds in dreams are always a means of representation for a secret). Resistance here was focused on the transference and warned me against expecting associations from below. Aware of the danger of offering an interpretation *in vacuo*, I waited until he gave me an opportunity to intervene. Only when he ruminated about the doctor in the dream having no time for him, did I say, "Turn it around."

By way of affirmation, he excluded me with a silence which lasted for the remaining half-hour.

A week later, John brought a dream with similar content.

It was literally about analysis. Instead of being here, the office was in Washington Heights. I was down by the river and had to climb a hill. The way was through a poor neighborhood. I was five minutes late. After all the climbing, I got to the wrong street.

He saw nothing terribly mysterious about the dream. He couldn't get where he was going. He'd had a bad weekend, "been in a daze, felt stubborn, thrashed around with non-feelings. . . ." He felt wrong and stupid in the dream. "There I go, half-and-half about everything. Everything is in a nothing position."

I repeated his last statement, saying, "When you say 'no,' nothing can happen. You say 'no' to me." After a brief silence, "That's what I'm saying to everything. I tell myself to do something, but I can't make myself do it. I can't say yes. It's pervasive. I feel as though I were in prison. Hell, I might as well shut up. I'm not getting any better; if anything, I'm getting worse."

I privately disagreed. His defensive insouciance was no longer proving tenable. Depression, a far healthier development, was taking its place.

"It's getting clearer how stubborn I am," he continued, "but nothing seems to happen to change it. I seem to be telling you that you're not doing me any good. In the dream it wasn't clear how I got to your office. I stopped too soon; which is obviously what I do here."

The interpretation of the last of the dreams could be specific because interpretation of the earlier dreams had prepared the way.

Every favorable turn in the analysis of masochistic patients automatically activates an archaic superego which, drawing on aggressive energy, introduces formidable barriers to progress. With each prospect of improvement in the treatment, resistance creeps out anew in the form of increased suffering. The negative therapeutic reaction may have other sources as well—clinging to infantile satisfactions, for instance—but its superego provenance is a potent factor in creating resistance.

During the course of a long analysis, Paul D. had married, become a father, and materially improved his professional position. Paul's history of negativism dated back to childhood when every feeding had been a battle with his mother. Later manifestations included procrastination, obstinacy, and parsimony, accompanied by an infinite incapacity for pleasure. Fantasies brimful of anguish attacked him whenever he was faced with the possibility of enjoying himself. Like so many patients, Paul tended to forget how much he had changed in treatment. Friends and relatives told him they saw signs of improvement, but his sessions continued to be filled with lamentation and complaints. He had this dream within days of telling me he had been promoted at work:

> I was in a hospital lying on a stone slab, covered with
> a sheet. I looked around and you were there.

He groaned that I would be the death of him. As a matter of fact, death was on his mind. His own, his wife's, his child's. He and I were at war with each other. Analysis had financially impoverished him. He had a business deal coming up later in the week. He expected to be "lacerated."

I was aware of Paul's tendency to transform whatever I said into the assault he unconsciously welcomed, to construe my interventions as "blastings." I therefore had learned to word my interpretations with particular care. Bearing in mind his recent success, his negative therapeutic reaction, and the dream image of the morgue (for the analytic situation), I said, "If it's better, it's worse, especially here." He summoned up a faint smile in recognition of his need to be miserable, and replied, "Yes, that certainly sounds familiar."

Intense negativism, however subtly couched, made obvious the extent of Paul's repressed aggression. He rarely heard me the first time, when he did hear he didn't understand, and when he finally understood he presented a counterargument. The morning he brought this next dream he was five minutes late which, when seen in conjunction with the dream, was tantamount to an association.

I am lying on a couch in this room. Instead of my head being on the pillow, things are turned around. My head is where my feet should be and my feet are on the pillow. The analyst too is at the opposite place, not in his usual position. He stands at the foot of the couch.

Here was a perfectly clear and graphic protrayal of opposition expressed in rebus form by location and position. How better to say, "Whatever you say or do, I take the opposing view"? Resistance was also conveyed by his use of the third person in referring to me. Taking into account his tardiness, I immediately offered an interpretation.

"I set one time so you make another. I prescribe one position on the couch and you take another."

"Huh. My wife is always telling me that no matter what she says or wants, I say or want the opposite."

I did not amplify my interpretation in terms of its oedipal connotations or with reference to its source in anal contests of will with his mother. I wanted to leave it on the level of resistance until his fight with me became ego-alien. Resistance here took the form of aggression in the transference.

5

The Dream as Resistance

The dream not only presents the forms and facets of resistance but may itself become a vehicle for the expression of the force which opposes analysis. As patients grow more aware of the role dreams play in analysis, they may unconsciously use them in the service of resistance. Such dreams, instead of illuminating, act largely to obscure and are therefore particularly inaccessible to interpretation.

The interminable dream is invariably a product of resistance. Should the analyst fail to pay attention to the details of a dream which consumes the major part of an hour in the telling, he would not be guilty of shirking his responsibilities. Analysis of the ostensible content, were it feasible, is not likely to be productive. Practical considerations of time alone preclude the possibility of investigating voluminous dreams. The same resistance that uses the dream to absorb an entire hour provides a variation by delaying presentation until the last few minutes. The analyst therefore need not feel much has been lost when a dream is reported too late in the session to be dealt with. He might in fact candidly acknowledge his inability to help very much when offered such dreams.

The formation of the interminable dream indicates an attempt to dream away anxiety and can be compared to the compulsive activity resorted to by those who seek to prevent eruption of disturbing thoughts and feelings. Prolonged dreaming can therefore be viewed as denial of unbearable anxiety, a substitute for reality. Indeed there are patients who say they feel apprehensive and inadequate when they have no dream to report.

The substitution of fantasy for reality may blur the distinction between the two. Patients sometimes devote so much time and attention to their dreams that we never hear about the significant events taking place in their daily lives. Exaggerated preoccupation with dreams converts the unreal to real and reduces the real to unreal.

Many years ago, when I was relatively raw and inexperienced, I had a disarmingly feminine patient who disparaged the duplicity of women who manipulated their men. From earliest childhood she had substituted fantasy for reality and lived in what she herself termed "a fictionalized style." She saw analysis as an esthetic accompaniment to her life, a dialogue which would produce fusion of the analyst with herself. She occasionally brought me sketches she had drawn to illustrate her feelings and the situations she created. Once, after telling me she had successfully resisted a temptation to masturbate, she reported this dream:

I saw the hands of a clock snipping off the hour of mid-
night as with a pair of scissors. A hand holding a knife
emerged from a closet. I approached it without fear and
it turned into a delectable fruit which I swallowed. I
then climbed a tree so I was invisible to anyone on the
ground. Far off in the distance I saw the tiny figures of
my mother and father slowly descend into the ground
and disappear from view.

She confessed immediately that she had fabricated the
whole thing. I vaguely recognized the incident as a piece of
acting out, but did not know what was operating to
produce it and accordingly made no attempt to deal with
the "dream." Were I confronted with a similar situation
today, I would unhesitatingly interpret the resistance that
produced this piece of artistic creativity. Even an invented
dream can have meaning if we choose to treat it as fantasy.
As an artifact, however, it merits consideration primarily as
a resistance which operates by making a mockery of the
analytic situation. My failure to interpret her behavior
correctly enabled the patient to evade exploration of her
impulse to masturbate which was in the background. It
undoubtedly also contributed to what followed. She consumed the next hour telling another dream and the session
after that in a reverie of composition:

A man bought and sold old dreams and placed a woman
under a spell to bring him her dreams which he then
marketed. The fantasy woman dwindled little by little
until nothing was left of her. The dream stealer stripped
her of everything; she gave him pieces of herself with
each dream.

In the service of resistance, then, dreams may be ex-
ploited as bribes, gifts, or as a means of distraction.

Moreover, the very act of dreaming and bringing the product to the analyst can constitute a source of satisfaction. The patient unconsciously equates the dream with creative ability, potency, or a good bowel movement and uses it to maintain a pleasurable state of infantile gratification rather than as a road to insight.

A patient, Simon E., whose rivalry with his father found expression largely in terms of money, had been bringing me a dream every day for several weeks. Such profusion, especially as it was attended by a conspicuous paucity of associations and an equally conspicuous delay in paying his bill, aroused my suspicions. When he introduced still another session with, "I had a dream ...", almost involuntarily, I interrupted, "Another?"

A silence ensued—a silence loud with his consternation. Then, "I must use them as an evasion, in place of something else."

"Money?" I asked.

After he corroborated this at some length, I added, "So you feed me dreams instead of money to keep me happy."

"Wow," he said and proceeded to tell me his dream, which contained incontrovertible evidence of repressed hostility.

> It was about you. You were smiling, but you were lying on a couch, leaning on one elbow. You were apparently sick. I put a pile of small white pillows over you to keep you warm and said, "I'm sorry." You gave that same peculiar smile.

I used as associations what he told me before the dream and said, "Those small white pillows you laid over me are what you sleep on, to dream, so you cover me with them."

Very soberly, Simon told me of a visit he had paid to his dying uncle, of his fantasy that his uncle would leave him money, just as he hoped his father would. "Your smile in the dream was my uncle's smile," he added.

In this instance a dream testified to the patient's use of his dreams as instruments of beguilement and placation.

The use of the dream to further the cause of resistance follows patterns laid down by character structure and the ego's methods of defense. The narcissistic personality often introduces itself by means of the dream which charms and captivates. The dream may even be prefaced with some remark equivalent to, "You'll like this one." Once having reported the dream, however, the narcissist will merely seek admiration for his product and want nothing further to do with it.

Markedly passive patients, either fearful of engagement or in expectation of magic, gain reassurance by coming equipped with a dream. The dream deposited, the homework done, they relapse into inactivity, hoping to leave the rest of the work to the analyst. Used this way, the dream is clearly one of convenience.

The obsessional character disorder is carried over into a typical style of recollecting, communicating, and working with dreams. Obsessional patients so interlard their reports of dreams with associations that the dream itself becomes lost to view. They break up the account into episodes, each isolated from the other, and spasmodically pursue each fragment with lengthy associations, making it difficult to know where the dream leaves off and associations begin.

Sometimes the patient, in an unconscious effort to ward off anxiety, will spontaneously offer an interpretation of a dream. His cooperation, however, is more apparent than real. Resistance here takes the form of providing the answers before all the questions that need to be asked of the dream can be put. By "interpreting" the dream before the analyst can, the patient effectively takes flight from its true anxiety-laden content.

Then too, many patients, exposed to popularized renditions of psychoanalytic jargon, convey resistance by using watered-down analytic concepts not only in their associations but in the manifest dream itself. If we overlook this pseudo sophistication, such dreams will appear deceptively ingenuous and straightforward.

"I have nothing to talk about today; my mind is an absolute blank." Without exception, remarks of this nature refer to something vigorously repressed, frequently masturbation or thoughts concerning the analyst. Jenny K., during the course of her analysis, had given up acting out in random, superficial affairs and had reverted to masturbation instead. Although she justified herself by saying that sexual deprivation demanded it, guilt and embarrassment at having to talk about her autoerotic activities interfered with her pleasure. She began a session with the preceding statement and followed her classic declaration with a twenty-minute summary of the news of the day. Then she presented a series of dreams, interspersing comments along the way which made it difficult to distinguish between dream and commentary. When I asked for enlightenment, she laughed and said, "You must be confused or else I am confusing you" (she was correct on both counts), and continued:

With X in a pastoral setting. We were just close, affectionate and loving, but no sexual passion or excitement. We embraced and kissed. I said, "It's the first time I've felt so close without having physical intimacy." Such a lovely feeling of closeness.

Then I was driving through a forest with my aunt. It was very dark. A bus came towards us, and because I couldn't find the switch to dim the lights, I had to turn them off. So did the bus. I wanted to turn the lights on again, but couldn't find the switch—it reminded me very strongly of groping for the clitoris. In the next part you were in it. We were lying in the forest and I was going to tell you what happened.

Jenny rambled along with a third dream, interrupting herself to observe how mixed up it was. I had already "stopped listening" and finally said, "Is there much more?"

"Not much. Why do you ask?"

"It seems like a lot."

"Well, I get the impression you think I am embroidering and adding things."

"Have you any ideas about the dreams?" I asked.

She thought the forest was undoubtedly symbolic, phallic. The trees were penises and all the dreams had to do with the clitoris. Again I interrupted, "Why last night?"

She was puzzled. She hadn't masturbated last night (first mention of the subject); she had slept soundly after taking a sedative, but no masturbation. She hadn't masturbated for a long time. Even when stimulated by sexual scenes in a play, she had not felt like masturbating. She did, however, touch her genitals when bathing and perhaps linger there.

Yesterday she had in fact rubbed an itch in her vagina but hadn't really masturbated.

"You know," I said, "how sensitive you would be to criticism of any kind if you had masturbated."

"That's true enough. And I did think you were being critical when you asked me about my dreams."

"At the beginning of the hour you said you had nothing to talk about. Masturbation is certainly nothing to talk about, isn't it?"

She laughed. It most certainly was not.... "God, in the first dream there was no sex with a man. In the second there was masturbation. I can just feel the correspondence between switch and clitoris now. What's wrong with me that I'm aroused by masturbation?"

Jenny's resistance was conveyed in circumlocutions, in somewhat self-conscious laughter, in the profusion of dreams, and in the manner of their presentation. My question, "Is there much more?" was designed to draw attention to her prolixity. Her guilt (over masturbation, with the analyst as transferred object) caused her to over-react. The high level of resistance that marked the hour deterred me from adding mention of another determinant for her opening comment, "I have nothing to talk about": an allusion to the female genitalia (Lewin, 1948b).

The question, "Why last night?" helped direct the patient's attention to events immediately preceding the dream and enabled her to see their relevance to it.

Particularly with dreams employed for purposes of resistance, analysis of defense takes precedence over interpretation of content. We demonstrate the use to which the dream is put by making plain the category of defense it serves. We underline the patient's need to prevent eruption of anxiety or to forestall recognition of dangerous ideas and feelings. As the case may be, we do best to make the patient aware of his lack of involvement, his passivity, or his desire to avoid reality.

6
Transference in the Dream

If the dream is the royal road to the clarification of resistance, it leads no less surely to the illumination of transference. The process of reviving impulses and fantasies involving significant figures of the past and re-enacting them with the analyst takes place silently and in the dark, precisely where the dream is at home and renders the greatest service.

When infantile attitudes are focused on the analyst through the dream, they are brought into the open and made more palpable. To deal with the tangible, the present, is always more meaningful for a patient than to contend with ghosts he cannot lay hand on. The dream gives concrete expression to transference (itself a concretization of powerful emotional states) and thereby removes analysis from the realm of the abstract. Dreams reveal the dreamer's prevailing conception of the analyst by the role they assign him. He may materialize as teacher, parent, officer of the law, spy, servitor, clown, driver of a vehicle, as president or monster. Correspondingly, the analyst's office may be transformed into an operating room, a prison, a museum of antiquities, a bathroom where duties are performed, a foreign land where strange languages are spoken, a restaurant, theatre, store, or library.

By conveying explicit information not otherwise available concerning the origin of the transference attitudes, the dream provides datelines for their genesis. The context of a patient's dream told me that the model for his current attitude came from the developmental level in which urethral and phallic urges predominated. The dream, a disguised wish to urinate on the analyst, made clear the original objects of the drive by condensing the figure of the analyst with that of his parents.[1]

Reactions to analysis and the analyst which are not carried over from the past, which are not new versions of an old relationship but are based on the situation as it actually exists, are also taken up by the dream. With dreams in which the analyst appears, it is important to distinguish between those presentations referring to him as he is and those endowing him with qualities carried over from earlier models. One dream can contain both, as with Hugo W.'s,[2] which expressed not only his resentment of his mother, transferred to me, but his response to an actual provocation on my part.

The analytic version of the child's relations to his parents carries the full complement of ambivalence inherent in its

[1] See dream, "Endless yellow stream" (p. 133).
[2] See dream, "Pushed parked car" (p. 71).

original edition. I have observed that many students regard positive transference as an encouraging therapeutic development but view negative transference as an evil standing in the way of progress. The real enemy is indifference. Any transference is preferable to none at all. Negative transference need not bring the work of analysis to a halt any more than positive transference automatically facilitates its progress. Either aspect can be the vehicle of intractable resistance.

The handling of dreams that contain transference elements depends on our appraisal of the patient's ego state. When we think the patient, aided by a critical estimate of the intensity of his own reaction and of its ego-alien, improbable nature, is on the verge of making a connection between past and present, we supply the necessary intervention to complete the process already active in him. The therapeutic value of transference demands, however, that we exercise caution in interpreting it to the patient. Unless interpretation can help deal with a defense, clarify a genetic development, or reconstruct a past experience, gratuitous emphasis of transference may disturb its delicate balance and interfere with its evolution.

Development of transference in analysis runs a course parallel to the controlled regression that the process of analysis invites. We may follow this regression through every level of development, along with the transference manifestations appropriate to each level, by observing the patient's behavior in the consulting room, his mood states, fantasies, anxieties, phobias, somatic manifestations, and characterological defenses. The dream, however, offers us correlative information that illuminates regressive developments with great definition. Not infrequently, dreams will even introduce the regression.

Olive L. was in her late forties when, following the death of her mother, she came for help, complaining that she was undecided about continuing her career as an editor of children's books, was worried about her inability to control her eating—which was making her corpulent—and was generally at odds with herself. Her only daughter, whom she had brought up herself after separating from her husband twenty years ago, was now married and gone. She lived alone, contentedly enough. But she had great difficulty in getting up in the morning, keeping her apartment tidy, and paying her bills. She tended to let things go. She was afraid of becoming "an old lady in sneakers." An older sister, a maiden lady, was hypochondriacal like their mother, and she did not want to become like either of them.

At first she took a dim view of lying down on the couch: she rather liked looking at me and watching my facial expressions. On the couch, she assumed a fetal position, curled on her side with both hands and feet suspended over the edge of the couch so that they almost touched the floor. She complained about losing control while lying down—she minded having it slip away from her.

During the hour she fell silent in a manner I could almost palpate—a contented, comfortable silence that was a presence rather than an absence—even though she somewhat plaintively wondered why she should come here and talk to herself when she could do that at home. When she did break her silences (which, I admit, I was impatient with and took for manifestations of withholding and resistance until I understood them) it was to speak, as she did not usually, with the unmistakable inflection of the part of the country from which she had come. I began to better appreciate the nature and provenances of this nonverbal communication when she told me she had started to lose track of the time—the days and hours—since coming to analysis, and of growing unaccountably sleepy when she lay down here, sometimes on her way here. It felt like "nap-nap" time to her. Once, she reported, she found herself with the key to her apartment in her hand as she was about to ring the bell to my office.

Whether because of an induced somnolence in myself, a counteridentification, I cannot say, but with all these observations before me, I still did not fully comprehend the nature of her behavior until she presented me with a series of dreams, starting with a recollection of one she had before she came to treatment:

I am sitting in the branches of an apple tree. I see far over the horizon at a great distance, as from the wrong end of a telescope which reduces everything to tiny size. I see beautiful tiny trees and flowers....

She had no associations, but, listening, I heard the transcript of her longing for the long ago—things seen at a distance as the means of representation for time in the past.
Now she dreamed:

I am asleep, but just awakening. On the floor beside the bed is a new-born child. It is a large baby and talks. It crawls into the fireplace.

She reported sensations about the mouth and the dwindling body experiences associated with falling asleep, that revived the situation of the child nursing at the breast (Isakower, 1938), occurring now on the couch. She remarked that she felt hungry and wanted to go to sleep. Although the hunger and "nap-nap-time" sleepiness had already been in evidence in the analytic hour, and I had commented on it, it had made no impression on her. When I connected her present feeling, the dream, her sleepiness and silence, "Your feeling here seems to repeat one you must have had when you were very little," she responded with a series of dreams, over a number of days, in which she was in restaurants, her childhood bedroom, and the following:

I was riding in a bus, all alone. It entered a moving-picture house, one of those old movie palaces of the thirties. It went down a side aisle with me, while I looked contentedly at a Greek frieze on the other side.

Even as she was telling the dream, she looked across at the relief of Gradiva hanging on the wall above the fireplace in my office and at the Greek vase standing beneath it. But all she spoke about was of wanting to sleep and eat, of feeling like a large baby when she was here.

Olive L.'s reaction to interpretations was to digest them in silence as though to indicate that she did not wish to be disturbed by them or to be intruded upon. But subsequent dreams and her gradual assimilation of them indicated her awareness of what was happening. After the following dream,

I am clad in a white gown that little girls wear to a child's birthday party. I feel so pretty.

she reflectively put together what had been going on for weeks, and said, "I seem to be going back in my dreams, all the time. And time is suspended, so I don't know one day from another, or care, for that matter. When I'm here, I feel as though my nurse should be dressing me in my snowsuit; I should be playing on the floor with my dolls; I should have my afternoon milk and crackers and cocoa with a marshmallow in it. Yesterday I was sitting doing nothing, just letting things wait, when I thought of my arrested development. What do you do about that? Do you suppose this had to do with my interest in children's books? Is that why I became an editor of children's books?"

Her acceptance was a measure of the analyst's acceptance. When I stopped demanding of her that she be verbal, when, with the dream's assistance, I understood the manifestations of the ego state induced by regression in the analysis, she responded by providing further dreams making matters even more explicit and meaningful to both of us. If we interpret dreams that herald the onset of regression in terms of passivity or resistance, we make the work of analysis harder for patient and analyst and retard its progress through misunderstanding of the inevitable unfolding of the timetable of development.

I have mentioned that transference, positive or negative, may become a source of intractable resistance—that the two can go hand in hand. Unconscious infantile-drive strivings may invest the transference with such intensity that they completely obliterate the reality of the analytic situation and vitiate the therapeutic alliance. If the work of analysis is to proceed at all, such transference, with its resistance implications, must be interpreted without waiting for optimal conditions. When transference takes this turn, the dream can help by giving advance warning of the need for interpretation before the patient acts out the ultimate resistance by leaving analysis.

Considering the high standards he set for himself, Daniel F. betrayed remarkable negligence with respect to the most elementary obligations. I was encouraged to see that his carelessness did not extend to analysis. He paid my bill promptly and kept his appointments with gratifying steadiness. At the same time, he persisted in asking me for advice and seemed incapable of any contact with his unconscious. We had worked together long enough, when Daniel brought this dream, for me to have discovered that his mother had catered to his every need.

> I was riding around in a little red car. It sputtered furiously. A man passing by said it needed fixing. I knew it. He got down to examine it and told me it leaked in many places. I didn't do anything.

He said his car actually did need attention but he had not yet got around to taking care of it. He then discussed at some length a financial problem that was troubling him and added, "I'd appreciate any comment you might care to make."

I was thoroughly accustomed to such phrases from him, but this time I answered, "You want me to fix it for you, to take care of your affairs, just as your mother did, without your having to exert yourself."

A long, reflective silence followed, a silence composed of doubt and hope that I would say something further.

Finally, he repeated his earnest wish that I would interrupt him as often as possible to give him my ideas on the subjects he brought up. A few weeks later Daniel brought this dream, typical for patients in analysis.

> I was at home in my pajamas. The bell rang and an analyst walked in. I was surprised to see him but thought, "Since he's here already he might as well stay."

In his associations, Daniel alluded to the inconvenience of fitting the analytic hour into his complicated daily schedule.

"How much more convenient," I said, "if you didn't have to come here, if I came to your home instead."

His dream was an almost naive expression of the sort of convenience he expected from me—the sort to which his mother had accustomed him. Because I was still in doubt concerning the quality of his object relationships, this dream gave me hope for the future.

After more than a year in analysis, Jenny K. complained that sexual abstinence made her feel dull and deprived. Analysis had taken away the one pleasure that made life worth living, and if that was what analysis did, she wanted none of it. She charged me with the responsibility for her unhappiness and castigated me vigorously for not helping. Interspersed with storms of abuse were brief intervals of contrition. During one of the abusive periods, she dreamed:

> I was having intercourse with one of my former boy-friends. I knew he was unhappy over another woman and

> I said, "I'd like to comfort you." But it wasn't true.
> I wanted the sexual pleasure for myself; I didn't really
> care about him.

She had been tempted to masturbate before going to sleep and had argued to herself that she was entitled to do so because she had no man to satisfy her. She nevertheless refrained and thought of blaming me for her frustration. With a small laugh, she said, "It's all your fault. I wanted to dump the problem in your lap."

After attributing her fatigue, insomnia, and other symptoms to sexual tension, she fell silent (an augury that thoughts of the analyst were unconsciously interfering). Then, "I feel I need a push from you; if I had a man I wouldn't have to masturbate."

"The man who gratified you in your dream belonged to another woman," I answered, "and you just said I was the one responsible for your masturbating."

Suggesting that the oedipal implications of another woman's man were not lost on her, Jenny said she was struck by the realization that men who attracted her and whom she wanted to seduce were either married or otherwise unavailable. She had to admit that when she thought of masturbating last night she had an image of me. Strangely enough, the room in the dream had been full of light, just like my office.

Three days later, Jenny began by telling me how pleased she was because her boss praised her work. She noticed, though, that there were others in the office he seemed to like better. She spoke of her foolish mother who didn't understand the currently accepted freedom in premarital and extramarital sexual relations and who was intolerably stuffy on several other counts. Only then did she mention she had a dream to report.

> I am at a dance; the setting is very erotic—Greek and Roman rooms, very festive in color. I am dancing. I have an assignation with a man for later, but I'm reading magazines to put it off. I'm proscrastinating, holding off what I know is to come.

She found the dream pleasant, although at the same time it made her feel frustrated and unfulfilled. Sex, which she was both anticipating and avoiding, was in the future: Long pause, then, "There is something brewing [pause] here."

The Greek and Roman objects in my office, visible from the couch, the reading of magazines which she did while she waited for her appointment, together with her wish to be the favorite "at the office" and her annoyance with her mother, all added up. In view of the earlier dream and her remark, "something is brewing here," my decision was for no intervention. I did not want to interfere with further development of the transference which was only moderately disturbed by resistance (indicated by the delay in reporting the dream). The erotic implications were producing anxiety, but not of paralyzing proportions.

Some two months later, Jenny explained there would be a delay in paying her bill and then presented this dream:

> I was in a department store, either working there or buying something. A man came in, talked prices and looked at a series of figures on a chart. He said something about my having a lot of work—two full jobs— how did I do it. Also something vague about money.

> Then I was with Jason Robards. He was playing piano
> and singing a love song to me. He said he loved me. It
> was wonderful. I wanted to tell him I loved him but
> couldn't say it.

Jenny thought I looked like Jason Robards. She compared
herself with a friend, also in analysis, who was always
furious with her analyst and couldn't imagine herself ever
caring for him.... She had been thinking of how hard she
worked and yet she never seemed to have any money. She
certainly envied people who did.

"If I loved you, you wouldn't have to pay your bill at
all," I said.

She thought money certainly made things very impersonal. Of course she wished I cared for her.... I must be
very rich—why did I charge such high fees? Her parents
were always offering to help her out but she hated to take
money from them. She often daydreamed of my making
special dispensation for her.... Her mother was lucky to
have a husband who could provide so liberally and give her
everything she wanted.

At roughly this time, Jenny reported a dream and made a
slip which she totally disregarded in her associations,
thereby calling attention to its significance.

> I was walking down a lane in the middle of a beautiful
> green field. I thought how nice it would be to live here.
> An adolescent came along in a car and started to ring
> his bell.

"Ring his bell?" I asked.

> It made a nice sound. A man came out of a house and
> said, "What's doing that?" Then he walked off with me,

putting his arm around me. He excused himself to go to
the bathroom, but it seemed he used a woman's toilet.
I wondered if he were mixed up about his sex. He asked
me if I was married, and I said, "Yes, five times."

Whatever else the dream referred to, I knew at once it
had to do with transference. The "green field" had, on
previous occasions, referred to my couch and, with the
ringing of the bell, clearly alluded to analysis. Jenny,
however, ignored these elements and addressed herself to
the question of the man's sexual identity. She wondered if it
had to do with her own confusion of sexual roles. I
recognized in her pedantic inflection and choice of words
the intellectual quality of her associations and interrupted
her.

"You are already familiar with all this."

She agreed and said she felt awkward and constrained
about something.

"The ringing of the bell?" I asked.

"That was strange. I meant horn of course. Could they
have been church bells?"

"They were not church bells."

She had absolutely no idea.

"The bell you ring when you come here," I said.

"Oh my!" Pause. "And the music it made which the man
so enjoyed."

"The beautiful music you want to make here," I added.

She would consider her analysis over if only she knew she
was pleasing me. For several weeks she had been feeling she
had not been doing her best. She so wanted to do everything right.

"Why the five times married?" I asked.

Well, the day before she had been comparing notes about

analysis with a friend and had thought she might do better if she could come five times a week.

While listening to her dream, I had thought of the precept which states that, with analytic patients, dream references to time or times have to do with analytic time. I had wondered at her "five times" because she came only four days a week. Without her associations, I might still be wondering.

When George G. brought the following dream, the transference existed on the most primitive developmental level, with him the soiling, wetting, nursing infant and myself the mother with a penis. This arrangement met with his complete satisfaction. The pleasure his analytic sessions gave him was marred only by my failure to talk more than I did. When he introduced the dream by saying he remembered "just a bit of it," I gave his comment the full weight of an association.

> I see the top floor of an apartment house. I am not
> sure whether I'm just looking on or being active in
> the dream. There is a stuffed-up toilet.

He recalled that months ago, here in this office, (the top floor of an apartment house), something he had said or done had made me say, "You behave as if this office were a toilet." Yesterday at work he had gone to the toilet but found it stuffed. He asked a colleague where he could find another bathroom. He was aware of his tendency to wince whenever he had to say "toilet." While waiting for the toilet to be repaired, he thought of moving his bowels in the sink. Yesterday his wife had been furious with him. He had promised to do something, then forgot as usual and had to be reminded, but still didn't do it. He liked to linger on the toilet. He used to love sitting there when he was small while his mother read to him to get him to move his bowels.

"Yesterday," I said, "you asked me to talk to you. You wanted to hear me speak. You want me to do for you what your mother did, while you are on the toilet here."

George told me that the night before, after intercourse, he had retired to the bathroom, sat on the toilet, held himself in for as long as he could, and then farted copiously, moved his bowels, and savored the resulting smell.

"You were stuffed," I said, "like the toilet in the dream."

He had had fantasies of my going to the toilet and soiling myself. He frequently soiled his pajamas in bed and had impulses to defecate on the floor. In the midst of these associations, he had a sudden urge to go to the bathroom.

With the help of the dream, one of the determinants for George's passivity and withholding could be traced to its genetic sources in the mother-child relationship.

Several months afterwards, George greeted me with uncharacteristic eagerness and the equally uncharacteristic news that he had two very important dreams to tell me. He'd had the first one on Saturday night.

> I am with a friend's mother who resembles mine. She shows me through a house and opens the door to a room which, she tells me, is the one her husband died in. It makes me uncomfortable.

He observed that in actuality he had visited the friend's father when he was dying and recalled having been affected as he bade him goodby. On Sunday night, he dreamed:

> It was you and me. I was coming to see you but your office was different. A girl was waiting to see you in the

hallway. You told her to make an appointment with your secretary. She was about seventeen and cute. You were friendly. I said, "I don't mean to cause you trouble." You said, "Excuse me," and went in to attend to a new couch you had. You were wearing white pants, very tight, up to the waist, no belt and a sport shirt like Belafonte. I was surprised and thought it inappropriate. You changed in the office and put on a tie. The couch was enclosed in a box like an elongated violin case. You started to work on a pole and a rope to lift the couch into the office. I admired how muscular you were. You did most of the work. I tried to help, holding on to the pole which got bigger and bigger.

He had recalled the dream while sitting on the toilet in the morning. At the same time, he noticed a discharge. At first he thought it must be left over from intercourse, but then decided it came from the dream though he didn't remember any sexual excitement in the dream. Funny, his saying "discharge" instead of "emission," as if he were talking about a woman.... Yesterday he had visited his father and been very critical and uncomfortable with him. While helping him move a television set, he worried about injuring himself. His father didn't have a tie on.... The dream made it easier for him to talk about the discharge and other things.... Last night he passed my house and talked to his wife about me.... How much better analysis was now than in the beginning. How different he felt toward his father from the way he felt toward me. That pole getting longer reminded him of a penis of course. He had enjoyed intercourse last night; his wife masturbated him, which was what he liked best.... The girl in the dream reminded him of having heard me say good-by to a woman outside my office one day. He wished I would be as friendly with him. A friend of his seemed to have a much warmer relationship with his analyst than he did. Right now he felt himself getting an erection. He wondered if, in the first dream, the dying man was me. He could talk to me so much more freely than he could to his father.

Here is a classic example of dreams used as gifts: he had "two very important dreams to tell me," had recalled them while on the toilet, and consumed a good part of an hour reporting them. George's assiduous and painstaking inventory of every part of the dream, his eagerness, made me wonder whether an element of contrivance, of something rehearsed did not lie beneath the facility, unusual for him, in associating. (A week later he alluded to his fear that I might throw him out because he wasn't working hard enough.)

I did not intervene. Notwithstanding evidence of resistance, the hour constituted an advance. He had overcome his passivity to the extent of bringing me a gift and producing associations. I did not wish to discourage this by drawing his attention to the numerous manifestations of developing transference or, for that matter, to the homosexual and oedipal elements in the dream.

The threat posed by the emergence of a patient's unconscious homosexual drive derivatives complicates development of the transference when patient and analyst are of the same sex. In dreams that pick up transference expressions of latent homosexuality, the dream work disguises either the people or the affect involved. As John Y.'s homosexual impulses began unconsciously to turn toward me, they were vigorously denied and acted out elsewhere. At this time he introduced a session by saying he had had a dream unlike any he had ever experienced.

> It was in the kitchen of a house in the country where I lived as a child. A woman was with me; we might have been married or were going to be. It was all so familiar and comfortable. She puttered about silently, then started out the door, holding a flour sifter which made a whirring noise. Suddenly, to my own surprise, because it came right out of me, without premeditation, I said, "But I love you, I do." She didn't seem a bit surprised or disturbed and, as though accepting it, said very quietly, "I know," and continued what she was doing. I woke up with the pleasantest feeling I can remember having.

He tried to connect the woman with those he knew but failed to satisfy himself that anyone qualified. (I remembered that a few days before, in reference to a discussion of his remoteness from people, he had described analysis as the only place he felt understood and accepted for what he was.) After he made further, vain efforts to connect the dream with his recent activities, I reminded him that yesterday, when he had objected to the "whirring noise" of my air conditioner, I had answered by saying, "I know." I also reminded him that yesterday I had had occasion to "go out" the door for a moment, and then asked, "Why do you suppose it must be a woman you refer to in your dream?"

He bridled. "Do you mean something homosexual?"

"We don't have to accept what the dream presents on its face as the last word."

"Well, maybe I'm taking it the wrong way."

Additional associations concerning the treatment situation drew John to conclude that everything in the dream, especially the atmosphere of acceptance and the quiet, "I know," pointed to analysis.

"It must be here," he said, still somewhat dubious.

"It sounds like it," I replied, and the hour was over.

Repression of homosexuality had blinded him to the dream's several allusions to me. In calling these to his attention, I hoped to make John's involvement with me less ego-alien. His reaction to my cautiously worded intervention warned me against persevering in that direction. I did not allow myself to be drawn by his leading question; his sensitivity to the subject of homosexuality would have nullified anything I might have said. I had to keep in mind not only what I wanted him to know, but how much he was prepared to take.

It should be noted that the experience revived by the dream related to the mother-child dyad. The complicated structure of homosexuality includes among its sources the child's search for mother (we sometimes tend to forget that homosexuals mother each other), with all the dangers implicit in this attempt at reunion. The danger is augmented when a man is sought to perform mother's functions. In calling on me to mother him, John ran the risk of surrendering to a man. Lacking a bridge either by way of context or associations, I did not make the genetic interpretation but preferred to detoxify the threat posed by his involvement with me and to relieve the anxiety caused by its homosexual implications.

When she was not rejecting him altogether, Hugo W.'s mother either complained that he neglected her, quarreled with his wife, or reminded him of the great expectations she

111

had of him and for him. He defended himself against her oedipal invitation and her threat to his autonomy by erecting a barricade against all emotional engagement. Toward the end of an hour devoted to silence and random chattter that led nowhere, I said to him, "You keep yourself at such a distance you make it impossible for me to get near you."

As he rose from the couch, he gave me a look at once beseeching and bewildered, then made his exit as if he could not get away fast enough. The next day he began with a dream:

> I was in a place where people were dancing. The curious thing was that men were dancing with men, women with women. A man asked me to dance and I didn't know which of us was to lead. I felt something was expected of me. We got out on the floor and swooped around as if neither of us knew what he was doing.

Hugo's associations, characteristic of his need to maintain severe intellectual control at all times, remained rigidly rooted to the subject of dancing. He made no reference to the previous hour or to me. Finally, I reminded him of what I had said the day before. His response, eloquent for him, was a long, drawn-out whistle ending in "Oh, oh."

The transference was too tenuous for me to tell him he had interpreted my remark as a homosexual overture. Although his customary aloofness gave every indication to the contrary, the dream, in the context of his relation to me, said he was hungry for contact.

A few weeks later, Hugo started his hour by describing an engagement he was to keep directly after it.

"You are already on your way," I observed. He replied:

I've gone off again, which reminds me of my dreams last night. I couldn't remember them. Or rather, I ran away from them. They started to come back when I was in the bathroom, but I dismissed them by reading the paper. I do remember, though, being a prisoner of war.

He was terribly annoyed with his little girl. She had a way of playing off her mother and grandmother against each other and thereby getting just what she wanted from both of them. He particularly minded her gambit because it made the friction between the two women worse. He wondered, as a matter of fact, whether his daughter was as artless as she appeared.

I knew Hugo's inaccessibility provoked both his wife and his mother to anger with him and with each other. I also knew he was oblivious to the contribution he made to the family discord. I said, "Perhaps your daughter is not the only innocent contributor to that situation."

"I don't understand what you mean."

"You sound as artless as your daughter."

Hugo admitted he had usually been able to get what he wanted from his mother by feigning sickness or pretending not to understand. He had always been well aware of his duplicity and even rather proud of it.

I wondered whether his dream was in any way connected with his playing dumb and said, "That dream of yours. Perhaps if we knew a little more it might help."

He recalled an experience he had had in the army. His ineptitude had caused him to be removed from the front line. Out of the danger zone, he had a daydream of being taken prisoner of war. Then he would look like a hero without any effort on his part. He conceded that his ineptitude in analysis seemed to have a corresponding intention.

Bringing him back to the dream was a chance I took which paid off. Here the merest fragment of a dream contributed to the analytic dialogue. For "I was a prisoner of war," read: the victorious captive, or how I won the war in prison.

Simon E. was an accepted resident of a fashionable suburb, had an attractive, devoted wife and several satisfactory children, but suffered from a feeling of general inadequacy. While he was acquiring his professional training and gaining recognition, his older brother joined their father in the family business. Simon resented the fact that his brother made more money than he, that he got along so well with their father. He saw his brother as a successful man of the world with never a glimmer of self-doubt or inner questioning. Simon was nagged by a sense of utter failure. He nevertheless liked to think of himself as congenial and unassuming, an assessment to which his friends and acquaintances would have readily subscribed. With his family, he was something else again, subject to sudden and unaccountable rages so intense they left him shaking with fear and remorse.

In analysis, his initial air of amiability yielded, with the development of transference, to one of sullen resentment. He never attacked me, but spent hour after hour in vilification of his parents and brother. This dream was one of a series he brought while working through his sibling rivalry in the transference:

> I was a child in the country in a bedroom with other children and a woman. She was annoyed with me,

wouldn't have anything to do with me. I wasn't wanted. She told me to keep away from other children who were playing with their toys. I was hurt, felt excluded, and thought I must be annoying to everyone. I tried desperately to get back with the kids and be accepted, but it seemed unlikely.

He emphasized the distress he experienced in the dream —a devastating conviction that he was unloved and unwanted—and then added:

In the dream I left the room and wandered down a cold gray road. I saw a man coming toward me. We recognized each other. I told him how I had been excluded. I was looking for logs to build a fire and it reminded me of camp.

He sighed deeply. He had just heard that a senior member of his firm had bypassed him in assigning some work. He worried a lot about what people thought of him. . . . A girl at the office had been making advances and, although he wasn't interested, he knew how hurt she would be if he rejected her.

"You know how she feels just as though it were happening to you," I said.

Yes, it was terribly important to him that he be accepted. . . . Yesterday he'd had the thought that I didn't like him as much as I did my other patients.

The "cold gray road" confirmed the transference aspects of the dream (the walls of my office are gray). Desolation of such magnitude underscored the probability of its having more than one source—an early childhood situation as well as the analytic one onto which it had been transferred. Rather than offer a genetic reconstruction which would have given him an intellectual loophole, I preferred to let him experience, in the transference situation, the depression he could not, in any event, be spared. I merely affirmed its presence by recognizing the identification he made with the rejected girl.

A year later, Simon had a dream with similar affective content. The work accomplished during this interval permitted a more concrete interpretation. In spite of a satisfactory transference and working alliance, he had been speaking sporadically of leaving treatment. He had the following dream after having been home ill for two days.

> In this office. You said to me, "It's no use, we can't go on. You just are not working hard enough." Then you told me you spoke to your father to get me to work harder. You shook your head as if to indicate things just won't work. I felt awful; I pleaded with you. I felt abandoned, empty, my whole life was crumbling. What would I do? Then I walked out and saw some other patients. I felt far more than excluded; much more intense than that. The main feeling was one of terrible despair and loss.

Since having the dream, he had thought of nothing else. It was obviously connected with the missed sessions. . . . He had been confined to bed on doctor's orders, so his absence was perfectly legitimate. He had to admit he felt relief at staying home, enjoyed being waited on. He wondered whether his illness contained psychosomatic elements and why, together with his relief and enjoyment, he had been nagged by a sense of uneasiness. And why a dream that left him so wretched, so desolate?

I linked the dream and associations with his repeated talk of stopping treatment and said, "When you stop analysis and leave me, you feel I have abandoned you."

Simon's grief and depression represented a characteristic reaction to loss of love. The dream and its affect carried the weight of the superego's response to jealous rage, originally directed at his brother and parents, subsequently transferred to me.

Six months later and just before a summer vacation, Simon brought another dream with transference elements distorted by reversal:

> I was in bed with another woman, not my wife, somebody strange and forbidden. There were two men; it was at camp. They grabbed me by both arms and were going to blackmail me. I got mad and wanted to call the cops. Then one of them tried to call a cop, too. The cops didn't respond.

His associations confirmed my impression that he seemed even more listless than usual. He felt depressed but could not account for it; nothing extraordinary was happening. He was looking forward to a vacation, to not having to come to his sessions with me. Although he didn't enjoy the preparatory details of moving to the country, he expected to have a good time once he got there. But everything seemed too much for him; nothing lifted him out of his lethargy, not even screwing. The dream made him think of a summer when he had been a camp counselor. One of the boys had insulted him, and he had retaliated by twisting the boy's arm and dragging him to the authorities. (I had already reversed the attack in the dream, a general rule that is always helpful.) He wondered why his depression was always worse when he was in my office. Today's was different: he felt more detached and could look at it a little. He was sure it had to do with my going away.

"You get depressed in this room in a very special way—blackmail—yours," I said.

Yes, it made him think of holding me back by the arm.

"It isn't just a thought," I added, "it goes deeper than that."

With sudden animation (probably owing less to the aptness of my observation than to my having spoken at all) he recalled another incident from childhood, when he was about ten. No sooner had his mother departed for the country for a few days' rest than he developed severe abdominal cramps. She returned at once to take care of him. He vividly remembered her solicitude, the way she crooned over him, and the immediate subsidence of his symptoms. He also remembered how his mother had always grown jittery and apprehensive at vacation time and made the whole family nervous with her preparations.

As if to dot the "i," Simon added one further association: the dream woman reminded him of my wife and provoked him to fantasy that I would say to him, "You want my wife," to which he would reply, "Cut that out, don't give me that stuff."

I did not interpret the oedipal content. Not only was it given near the close of the hour, it came as an afterthought and in the form of a disclaimer, bound up with resistance. It was, moreover, of secondary importance to his reaction to imminent separation. The anaclitic relation with mother, transferred to analyst, could be expected to reappear at a time of parting. Explication of the dream's reference to both his drastic holding action and to anger with me helped him recover earlier memories of rage and depression when mother left him and he was alone.

Don J., unmarried, uninterested in marriage, came to analysis when he was in his middle thirties after consultations with a battery of doctors had left a wide assortment of physical symptoms unexplained. Flamboyance characterized Don's life style. Very much the man about town, he groomed himself fastidiously, drank the best wines, dined at the best restaurants, and slept with the most glamorous women. His attempt to satisfy his need for sexual conquest amounted to an addiction but brought him no lasting pleasure. Don had a propensity for the melodramatic which, by the time he brought the dreams about to be cited, he was beginning to view with a more critical eye. Increased insight, however, had wrought little discernible change in his behavior. He continued to transform the drop of a pin into an international incident and to express himself in hyperbole. I therefore did not move to the edge of my chair when he introduced a dream by saying, "Doc, I had the wildest one last night. These dreams are killing me."

It was here. I was on the couch but I was sleeping. In my sleep I had a dream but it was blank. Then you were standing next to me saying, "We have to stop now." I woke up, realized I had slept through the whole hour, and got up woozily to go out. Even then I still knew it was a dream.

The idea of a dream within a dream, of dreaming he was asleep, was so strange, he'd never had anything like it before. . . . Lately he'd been feeling very strange altogether. More and more, everything he did seemed unreal. He had just been offered an important commission but didn't seize on it as he usually did; he even thought of turning it down although that would mean less money in the till. He felt he would sleep through the job. Neither it nor the money seemed real.

"You don't treat what you do here as real either," I said.

"I do feel that something is missing, that I'm leaving something out." (I considered this statement a sign of beginning self-awareness. I think it is represented in the manifest dream by the image of his waking up and "realizing" he had slept through the hour.)

To demonstrate his eagerness to cooperate, Don briefly expanded on my interpretation as if it had been his own, then lapsed into silence. Finally he said, "When I was a kid I always had to take a nap after lunch, supposedly because I had a bad heart."

"You take a nap after lunch here too, just as you did then," I replied.

In this instance the dream work used "a dream" to detract from the importance of a wish or actual past event that was being forcefully repudiated. Don's dream within a dream was a blank, representing his wish to sleep, satiated and passive at his mother's breast (Lewin, 1946, 1948a). His associations alluded to childhood sleeping patterns. The spoken word "stop" (his superego) condensed his father's interference with his first love affair and the analyst's current interference with the acting out of his oedipal fantasies. Then too, he could hardly have chosen a more effective means of "stopping" analysis than by sleeping through the hour (Lewin, 1953). In addition, his dream testified to the intimate connection between orality and sleep. He would sleep and dream through analysis as he slept as a baby after feeding and as a child after lunch, while the analyst-mother provided magical solutions by feeding him interpretations.

Patients often pick up our interventions and incorporate them into subsequent dreams. My transference interpretation of the afternoon nap constituted one determinant for a dream Don presented a few days later:

I'm in a bungalow where I lived with my parents in the summertime. My mother was ironing, but it was you, actually. I sat down on a green lawn in front of her and performed a little kiddie dance. Even in the dream I was aware of the word, exhibitionism. I thought, "I hope you—mother—see me and know how lonely I am." But you kept on ironing, looking down, not at me. I tried and tried to catch your eye. Everything seemed awfully quiet as though everything had stopped.

He did not refer to the hour just described, nor did I, although I had it in mind (the "quiet," the "green" lawn for my green couch, the temporal regression, all spelled transference). He told instead of his excitement last evening at the prospect of meeting a new girl—would she be impressed with him? He set out glasses, lowered the lights, turned on soft music—the works—all the while shaking his head and thinking, "How you do go on, and yet you have to do it, you can't stop."

"You came on for the girl just as you come on for me and as you did for your mother in your dream."

The seduction scene preceding the dream paralleled Don's attitude toward his mother as well as his expectations from me. Resistance had played its part in the first dream; transference interpretation led to the second. The latter reflected the ego's perceptive and synthesizing functions and also served to validate the earlier interpretation: it picked up the part dealing with transference as shown in its statement, "I hope you—mother—see me and know how lonely I am."

Any classification of dreams is, as I have said, arbitrary, artificial, and potentially misleading. A grouping of dreams under a transference heading (or any other, for that matter) does not do justice to the complexity of processes that enter into dream formation. All dreams produced during analysis contain transference elements. The principle stating that the person to whom a dream is told plays a role in the latent content applies equally well to the analyst.

We have dealt with transference-oriented dreams which occurred during the early stages of treatment and have noted the limitations of their interpretation. We have seen transference inextricably linked with resistance. We shall constantly encounter transference in the dreams still to be considered.

7
Anxiety and the Dream

While anxiety is an inevitable reaction to analysis, the anguish it creates, unless modified or kept under control, can be disruptive. With patients whose anxiety is a presenting symptom in the forefront of the clinical picture, we know to some extent what we are up against and can adjust our procedures accordingly. But where anxiety is deeply buried, we risk, in our ignorance, taxing the patient beyond his endurance by premature confrontations. When anxiety is clinically invisible, the dream—and frequently only the dream—will testify to its presence. The dream also tells us more about the balance between drive and defense and between ego and superego.

The endurance of anxiety in a dream is painful, even devastating. Once waking control is established, the ego, especially when supported by the psychoanalyst, can look at it in a different light. The dream, by concretizing anxiety and placing it in perspective, prepares the patient to bear distress in face of the upsurging unconscious. Interpretation permits him to countenance his anxiety at one remove, gives him a chance to view it a little more objectively, and alleviates his terror constructively by increasing ego autonomy. Associations to dreams leading to interpretation of anxiety extend the range of the ego's perceiving function, in the course of time expanding its limits of tolerance and thereby serving the ultimate goal of analysis: to enlarge the ego's capacity for synthesis and integration. Interpretation of the sources of anxiety in dreams provides a dramatic opportunity of demonstrating to patients the pathology produced by fantasy and by unconscious infantile drives.

We anticipate anxiety throughout analysis. Anxiety connected with conscious or unconscious conflicts that bring people to analysis will be exacerbated by anxiety that a venture into a new and totally unfamiliar experience usually arouses. Those interpretations I gave for early dreams which referred to defenses automatically took into consideration the presence of anxiety. Anxiety as the ego's response to a threatened disturbance of its equilibrium played its part in creating the dreams illustrating resistance. We have seen certain phases of the transference engender anxiety by their evocation of early anxiety-laden conflicts the patient had never been able to face and which were encountered and repeated in the analytic situation. Each interpretation of defense, each lifting of repression, each fresh exposure of the unconscious, each new adjustment (including termination of treatment), while necessary to progress, gives rise to anxiety until a new equilibrium is reached.

Whether we stress anxiety in our interpretations, allude

to it, or exclude all mention of it; whether we interpret anxiety, drive, or defense, depends on our estimate of the patient's preparedness. As always, we are guided by the compulsion of the drive and its proximity to consciousness, by the strength of ego and superego, by the state of the therapeutic alliance, by transference considerations, by the context in which the dream occurred. Once again, in lieu of rules, we are guided by our overriding objective, to make the unconscious conscious without introducing cause for renewed resistance.

After three years in analysis, John Y. still fiercely resisted all efforts to acquaint him with his unconscious. He habitually responded to my interpretations with a noncommittal, "Yeah," followed by an immediate change of subject. He associated by clinging to the manifest dream as though to depart from it were unthinkable and totally irrelevant. As I have said earlier, John dreamed freely enough and reported his dreams punctilliously but, this done, rejected them as having no significance. With a laconic New England reserve superimposed on an obsessive-compulsive neurosis, he managed, by deleting his associations of all affect, to deprive of meaning even his occasionally dramatic dreams. He introduced this dream by saying he had never dreamed anything like it before[1] and, as usual, could make nothing out of it.

Like I am a camera, observing but not participating. I am looking through the camera in a restricted place in a dark cave, filming a scene. I see a big scorpion which

[1] Compare this with his introduction to dream, "Love in a country kitchen" (p. 110).

someone outside is trying to kill. It was four or five feet long. The guy outside pushed sand into the cave with his hand and fist, rapidly pushing and pulling it in and out—so sexual. He pushed in a cold lobster tail with poison on it as bait so the scorpion wouldn't bite him. Jeez what a dream. I'm recording this match of wits. It's dangerous and unpleasant.

When he woke up he thought how full of sex the dream was. Where in hell did it come from? ... At lunch yesterday, with one of his girls, he engaged her in a teasing match. It was sexual, being mean about it, but without getting anywhere. She gave him a book which he read after he got into bed. It had to do with sex, especially the attractions of older women, and excited him so much he masturbated.

"Before the dream?" I asked.

Yes, he awoke during the night with an erection and couldn't get back to sleep so he masturbated. He had spent the evening as usual, calling various girls. Two of them were angry with him, which he found rather attractive. He had been unsuccessful with both.

"Unsuccessful?"

Yes, he thought he'd told me. He had premature ejaculations and had to satisfy them manually, feeling threatened throughout. He couldn't see any connection between the dream and anything else. The dream made him mad. It wouldn't turn out to be anything. But it was such a symbolized fear of sex. It wasn't exactly a horror dream— he wasn't in a sweat, didn't wake up as in a nightmare—but in terms of sex, the dream was enough to turn you off. That was how he was. Afraid of sex. He was mad at me for not saying everything would be O.K. The dream guy throwing sand in so as not to be bitten reminded him of throwing up a smoke screen on sex. It was literally the way he felt when he was having intercourse.

(I recognized the defenses set in motion by anxiety connected with masturbation and fear of castration, but until he was more specific in his associations, I limited myself to asking questions that would encourage him to keep going.)

After lunch in the girl's apartment they took pictures of each other—ah, the camera—as part of the teasing sex game that went nowhere. At one point he wrestled with her on the floor where he had her spread-eagled. He was beginning to think the dream had to do with her—her position reminded him of the scorpion.... There was something he couldn't get at. Odd that in the dream he should say, "I am a camera." ... The time he wasted with girls, not knowing what he was doing with them. He felt about the dream as he did about sex.

(His reference to irrational sexual activity suggested that he had achieved enough distance from himself to warrant my intervening.)

"You need to be so active sexually and keep so busy with the girls in order to prevent yourself from feeling uneasy about sex, but it comes out anyway."

It was obvious to him that the sex thing was good only if you felt easy about it. Just like in the dream, he did things he was uneasy about. But great, what else was new? ... The poison bait was odd. A small crab—oh yes, a woman at the office had said she felt poisoned by something she ate. Poison sounded so significant. "What the hell. 'Uneasy.' What a word indeed. So?"

"All right then," I said, "anxiety which is too painful to bear so you run away."

He recalled occasions after intercourse when he had

127

fantasies of a man attacking him. Once he had a chilling vision of stepping on a giant clam which held his foot in a vise until he drowned.... There sure was something crazy about screwing around this way....

In spite of John's intellectualizations which strove to drain off anxiety, his dream apparently impressed him. Whereas sometimes even seeing is not believing, a dream of this intensity cannot easily be dismissed, scorned away. His dream showed him something about himself he had not seen before (he had "never dreamed anything like it before").

The visual images of the dream, concretizing the abstract, lend a sensory surface to ideas which obsessive patients in particular, with their tendency to escape into abstractions, cannot help but perceive and register. By translating the problem into pictorial images, by bringing it alive, John's dream made clear to him how his frenzied sexual activities, including masturbation, were at once the cause and consequence of his anxiety.

A year and a half later, John was still acting out, still defending himself by isolation, but analysis and experience had exerted their influence. His defenses were proving less and less effective. Increasing anxiety bedeviled his acting out. He no longer dismissed his dreams as of no consequence. Here is one that impressed him particularly.

We—myself, people, animals, all mixed up—were coming along a river with big rocks carved with huge faces, fifty feet high, like the ones out west, very unusual. Now comes the part hard to describe. I seemed to be inside but still outside a large room. Among the animals was a fox or wolverine with reddish hair, like a pet dog. She seemed to have a litter; they looked like fat little cats.

The fox began to metamorphize, get bigger, stand on its hind legs, become like a sloth with long arms weaving about. She looked as if she was about to go out of her mind or have a fit. She seemed to have grown long claws and began to attack her own children, her litter, apparently under the misconception that they were made of spinach—Jesus what a crazy dream. She was out of her mind, attacking and ripping them up to get at the spinach. I said, as though she were my responsibility, "No, no, they're not made of spinach." The other people took no notice but I tried to stop her, she was so obviously out of her mind, attacking her own cubs, ripping them open to get at the spinach, really going to kill them. She ripped them open and blood spilled all over. I couldn't do anything. I was her friend. She followed me. I wanted to get away—how can anybody have a nutty dream like this?—and ran to my car, frightened. The thing was going mad for spinach. I woke as she was going to get me before I could get into the car.

He muttered, "Ah Christ," sighed heavily, and continued in his customary drone. Last night, working late, he felt lightheaded, nutty, couldn't focus his eyes properly. He hadn't done anything particular during the day except talk on the phone to some of the girls he knew. Oh yes, he did get sunburned at the beach with Z, "Hmm, that had to do with the claws."

John mumbled something so indistinctly I had to ask him what he had said. With obvious reluctance, he admitted to having masturbated the girl, Z. "The manual thing was like killing the girls . . . what about that damn spinach thing?"

I repeated his locution, "Thing?"—an intervention I frequently adopted to point up one of his unremitting isolating devices and to prevent him from depriving his associations of their true significance.

Yes, what kind of thing was that spinach—ripping the cubs to get at it? "It sounds like an absolute mockery. It was fantastic, horrible. I seemed to be identified with it."

(I noticed the hostile "mockery," the animal as fox, wolverine, and sloth—a condensation of images of himself in his sadistic, phallic role. I also noticed his superego evaluation, but in order not to interrupt, resisted the temptation to confirm his insight.)

He was disturbed by his casual sex with Z. It wasn't a good thing to do. He thought of the Arabs and their inability to learn a lesson. They needed to have it driven home to them—more punishment. What did that have to do with kids being ripped open, the spinach, the fox going crazy? She didn't know what she was doing, attacking. What was going on inside him? He must be real nuts but all covered over with his reasonable crap.... There *was* something yesterday, a major thing. His mother called. (This was his first mention of her in months.) They had a long talk. She asked if he was going out with many girls. He told her yes, but he wasn't getting married yet, if that was what she meant. She assured him it wasn't. There was something maternal about the going crazy in the dream. His saying "no" to the fox had just been a distraction, he didn't really interfere. He couldn't believe the animal could possibly do what she did, but she really did rip up those kids. He felt as if he were losing touch with reality just thinking about this thing.

"Thing again?" I asked.

"The dream."

To refuse him further access to denial I followed up with, "The thing inside you."

A pause. "Right." Another pause; I could almost feel the

idea being absorbed. Then, he was thinking of yesterday, Father's Day, and being given a present ... oh yes, "that stuff inside" him.

Once more from me, "Stuff?"

For sure it was inside him.... His mother had said, "Well, you can be glad you have your kids." And he had said it would be lousy if he didn't. He had meant to call his daughter, who sent him a card, but he hadn't done it. His son didn't send anything. Yes, by God, he had quite a few thoughts about the kids yesterday. There was something horrifying about the way he was acting lately, as if he had no troubles, being so casual, so uninvolved. He just thought of the expression, "I say it's spinach and the hell with it."

The succeeding hours confirmed the impact made by the dream. John had been unable to sleep for thinking about it. He consulted his childhood diary to see if the date of the dream corresponded to an early experience of some kind and found it coincided with the date his father had set out on one of his many trips abroad. The part about spinach would not leave his mind. It occurred to him that spinach had always been accounted something admittedly unpleasant but good for you. He anticipated me by adding, "That certainly sounds like a reference to analysis."

In associating to the dream about the scorpion, John explicitly denied his anxiety ("It wasn't exactly a horror dream, I wasn't in a sweat") and its contribution to his pathology. In the current instance, he felt and acknowledged his anxiety, and there was therefore no reason for me to stress it, especially as it was not interfering with his associations. I was content to direct my interventions toward his isolating defense with my queries about "stuff" and "things," supplemented by the single confrontation.

131

Early in analysis, before a definitive development of the transference, Jenny K. had mentioned her masturbatory activities with relatively little hesitation or embarrassment. When her erotic impulses began to focus on me, however, she could no longer deny or avoid the anxiety aroused by their oedipal implications. During this phase of treatment, she introduced an hour by complaining of discomfort at the onset of her menstrual period. She'd had rather a lot to drink the night before, and as she lay in bed afterwards, fondled her breasts which were tense and swollen. She started to masturbate but blacked out before she could have an orgasm. Then she had a nightmare.

> I'm in what was my parent's bedroom in the house I grew up in, only now it's my house too. I wake up too late to keep my appointment with you. I'm not upset about missing the appointment, but I do want to call and tell you I won't be in. I go to a phone but there are no numbers on the dial which has slots instead of holes where you put your finger. You have to feel around for them—it sounds masturbatory. Then the nightmare started. I got more and more anxious to reach you, but I couldn't remember your number, couldn't find it in the phone book, couldn't find it anywhere. The searching was anguish and woke me up, which was a great relief. I was so glad it was just a dream.

She thought missing her hour meant she didn't want to talk about masturbation. If she didn't come, she couldn't talk about it, just as in the dream she couldn't reach me. Last night she had been afraid I would be angry and punish her. "It's striking I could black out in the midst of masturbating."

I saw her syncopal attack as an equivalent for anxiety and said, "You have to put sexual thoughts out of your mind because they make you anxious when they concern me."

She recalled a previous occasion when she had blacked out in the midst of having intercourse. She'd been drunk then, too. She had never thought about it before, but having amnesia while sexually excited was pretty pathological.

My interpretation took account of the transference source of her anxiety, the defense against it, and the resistance it evoked. Within the week she brought a dream in which her oedipal impulses were directed toward me much more openly and were so interpreted.[2]

Anxiety generated by aggression may lead to the institution of defenses severe enough to paralyze the child and later the adult. When anxiety prevents the patient from facing his hostile impulses, interpretation of a dream can help him acknowledge and accept their existence.

Although Simon E. complained of feeling anxious both before and during his sessions, he rejected out of hand suggestions that hostility toward me and fear of my reactions were responsible. Then he reported this dream:

> I am sitting with you and your family at dinner. You are jovial and friendly. I ask if I may serve you some lemonade and pour a seemingly endless stream of yellow fluid into your glass, which seems never to fill.

I interrupted a long silence to ask if he had any ideas about the dream. He said he felt uncomfortable because, although he made a special point of emptying his bladder every day before he came in, a need to urinate persisted through the hour. . . . He had been comparing analytic procedures with friends of his who were in treatment. He

[2]See dream, "Wants to comfort her boy friend" (pp. 101-102).

wondered if I were really as competent as he had originally thought.

Previous attempts to confront Simon with his hostility toward me had obviously been premature and had merely given rise to more anxiety. The dream work's distortion in presenting a manifest content of disarming solicitude suggested the continuing pressure of his defenses. Direct interpretation of his aggression, therefore, would have been futile.

"You have to pee away your anxiety here," I said.

This led to further, somewhat less hesitant confession of the lengths to which he had gone in criticizing me and his reluctance to tell me about it.

The interpretation incorporated the symbol "yellow fluid," the anxiety, the transference "here," and only implicitly, the aggression. The next day Simon's uneasiness was even more apparent. In a barely audible voice, he treated me to an apathetic account of current events, finally trailing off into silence which I did not interrupt. That night he dreamed:

> I was riding with a friend of mine who is a reckless driver. He was speeding down a highway recklessly and I was in anguish. I could say nothing but I kept putting my foot down hard on the floor as though to put on the brakes and keep us from having an accident. I woke in a sweat.

In view of the preceding sessions, I knew repressed rage provided one determinant for the dream. Perhaps his associations would make an intervention relevant and appropriate.

Yesterday a man in his office proposed a course of action

he disapproved of, but he could not bring himself to say so—"I could say nothing about it." Later on, in spite of his efforts to keep it down—"putting my foot down"—he had lost his temper with the man over another matter. He had been upset all day; even his hour with me had been more disturbing than usual.

"You have to pee when you are here because you are afraid—afraid of losing control of yourself with me."

Somewhat hesitantly, Simon admitted he had been furious with me because of my silence. It seemed so heartless. He had wished for something awful to happen to me and got progressively more anxious at the idea of having to tell me so. "I guess I was the one headed for an accident, wasn't I?"

Although I was prepared to interpret his dream as soon as I heard it, Simon was not prepared to receive it. I had to consider the repression which made the dream necessary in the first place. By allowing him to review what he had experienced since the previous hour, I gave him time to acquire perspective, to recognize how he had displaced his rage. Only then could I confirm and round out the discovery which he, abetted by the dream, had already made. Interpretation of the dream broke a circular reaction (rage, anxiety, silence, rage) that might otherwise have gone on indefinitely.

Unconscious anxiety contributed to forming Roy L.'s dream in which a soldier lay castrated on a stretcher.[3] Six months later, Roy had another dream produced by the same conflict, but whereas in the earlier dream all traces of

[3]See dream, "Castrated soldier on stretcher" (p. 57).

135

affect had been eliminated, the second dream restored the full quota of affect associated with castration anxiety by terminating in a nightmare.

> I am lying in a room when suddenly the lights go out. I have the feeling something terrible is happening. I feel something over my face and can't breathe. I know I am going to die. I struggle, but there is nothing I can do.

He was obviously still within the grip of the dream as he told it, and plunged headlong into a highly emotional recollection of an early traumatic experience. When he was about five years old, he had been taken to a doctor's office to have his tonsils removed. After a long wait, the door to the operating room swung open. He saw an unconscious child being carried out and the doctor, his apron covered with blood, nodding toward him. He remembered being dragged "half-dead" with fear into the office, "nailed down to a chair," and having an awful-smelling thing clamped over his face. He would never forget that smell and "it was a long time ago."[4] All his life he had dreaded injury, illness, and disfigurement.

I remembered his early castration dream with its remarkably indifferent feeling tone and asked, "How old did you say you were at the time?"

"Five."

"And how old were you when you saw the boy with the mastoid scar, would you remember?"

"About the same age. That's right. Your question reminds me of that dream I had of the soldier lying on a stretcher with a scar like the boy's."

---

[4] This phrase appeared in his earlier dream, "Castrated soldier on stretcher" (p. 57).

We know that significant conflicts appear repeatedly during an analysis, presented from various points of view. In this instance, dreams presented one theme on two different levels at two stages of analysis. The first dream clearly represented castration but was conspicuously devoid of affect. Associations had led to the patient's anxiety-laden perception of another boy's surgical mutilation. In the current situation, anxiety was experienced directly in the dream, but associations led to the memory of a traumatic experience in another area—the tonsillectomy. Only the time factor remained common to both experiences and to the developmental stage of expectable castration anxiety. My interventions in both instances were preparatory, inferential, and only hinted at relationships and connections. They never explicitly referred to castration. I wanted to help the patient see for himself, to further the flow of associations, to deepen the analytic process, and to bring together the two levels of experience.

Months later, Roy's superego began to participate more overtly in the analytic dialogue. One evening he took an attractive girl to a concert. The florid images evoked by her physical proximity made it difficult for him to keep his mind on the music. He turned his attention to the audience but saw only lascivious visions of exciting women. In a final effort to control his thoughts, he conjured up the image of his stern father (a minister), mentally appealing to him to forbid indulgence in such abominable behavior. That night he had a dream:

> I was in a temple, church, or library. The stained-glass windows glowed in the dark. An organ started to play and filled the hall with sound. It got louder and deeper until it sounded like a growl. I was terrified. It seemed

to envelop and crush me, the sound did. I woke up sweating and shaking.

As he reinvoked the dream in reporting it, he shivered. He immediately connected the sound with his father's voice.

"Sexual thoughts are exciting," I said, "but they also make you suffer. You even ask to be told to stop so you won't have to feel so anxious."

"It was awful," he replied, "you certainly would think it was a warning." He added that when he was a child, he had constructed a complicated ritual to prevent himself from masturbating, a ritual that had included praying to God to make him ill if he persisted.

My interpretation emphasized the anxiety created by his sexual indulgence and hinted at the transference element (contained in the dream's "temple, church, or library," a reference that combined his father and myself). I made no academic reference to his superego or to his oedipal problem. Just as interpretation of defense so often takes precedence over interpretation of drive, so interpretation of deeper levels must yield to consideration of anxiety when it is of overriding importance—a precaution I failed to observe in the following instance.

For weeks Don J. had been trying to cope with a free-floating rage which reached out to family, friends, colleagues, and of course to me. Day after day he moaned how helpless he was in the grip of this overwhelming animosity. He labeled himself an animal, could not imagine why anybody tolerated him. Then he reported this dream:

There was an awful beast, a monster, with me in a meeting hall. Just the two of us. The beast was half me, like a werewolf, just an animal. I don't know whether it squeezed me or I tried to strangle it, but urine kept squirting out of us and began to cover the whole floor. I woke up in a sweat.

Don ignored the dream to detail fresh examples of his flying off the handle. I read the dream as a phase-specific expression of rage, having its genesis in phallic competitiveness represented as urination, and said, "Wouldn't it feel good to soak everybody, to pee on everybody, as you must have wanted to do a long time ago to express your feelings."

In sharp contrast to his usual stream of volubility, he received this with a prolonged silence. As I look back, I think it would have been better had I given more consideration to his anxiety. Perhaps Don's silence indicated that he was not prepared to assimilate my intervention, that it was too precipitate. He certainly gave me no evidence that my interpretation had reached its mark. Sometimes we grow so accustomed to the hysterical components of a patient's personality that we fail to do justice to the layers of anxiety embedded therein. By the same token, the rigidly controlled patient with his unvarying superficial self-possession, may lead us to underestimate the explosive forces that required the erection of this barrier to and safeguard against anxiety.

As analysis of his defenses began to upset his lifelong reaction formation of exaggerated politeness and extravagant attention to protocol, Hugo W. voiced concern at the frequency with which he was losing his temper, especially with his small daughter. She was his only child and kindled in him a tenderness he felt for few people. He was, however, terribly disappointed by her physical timidity, particularly as he set great store on athletic prowess. The more he disparaged her fearfulness, the more apprehensive she grew. In exasperation, he scolded her, but ended up wondering whether his irritation had been justified. After one such episode he had this dream:

> My daughter was gone. She was staying with friends and hadn't come home. Then it seemed she had been away for several days. I sat on a beach watching a sailboat in which her friends were sailing, but she wasn't there. Then I was home, in a sweat, and awoke, thinking, "You have nothing to be afraid of, she's back in her bed."

When he repeated, "I can't stand her fearfulness," I said, "You would like to have nothing to be afraid of. She reminds you ..."—"of myself," he interrupted and continued with a long description of his physical cowardice.

"Anxiety isn't pleasant to have around, so you don't want it near you," I said.

"Anyone who can't keep his shirt on makes me uneasy. I don't want to know about it. Of course that must be it. I can't stand seeing it because it's in me. Otherwise why should I mind so much?"

The great danger that threatened Hugo's prized self-possession and exposed him to anxiety was his deeply repressed rage. I confined my interpretation to his characterological defenses against any eruption of emotion. While it was possible to show him how his dream referred to fear, hitherto strenuously denied, he was not yet prepared to hear of the sadistic impulses which lay behind the fear. I considered even an intellectual acceptance of an interpretation at this time, better than none at all.

Three months later, after saying he had lost all sexual appetite for his wife or anyone else, Hugo introduced a session with the breezy announcement, "Last night I fucked my wife." I knew he was concerned about impotence, and this show of virility stirred my suspicions. I was, moreover, struck by the boldness of his expression and said so. With unwonted cockiness, he described how, on the spur of the moment, he had taken the initiative and been assertive. He quickly got an erection and maintained it; intercourse was prolonged and he decided to have an orgasm without worrying too much about his wife. Sometime during the night he had a dream:

> I was in a bus. If I did something—I don't know what—stand up, sit down—it was vague—"it" would get knocked off. It was as though there were two of "them"—I don't know what.

In the silence that followed, I reminded myself that phallic duplication (two "its") was a warding-off of castration. Hugo broke the silence with one of his characteristic defensive maneuvers: he fled from the dream into an extensive digression related to his work. When he finally returned to the dream, he saw no connection between the dream and what preceded it.

"After intercourse you dream of 'it' being knocked off," I said, "what is 'it'?"

He conceded it could be nothing but the penis, and added, "After successful intercourse I always worry whether I'll ever be able to do it again."

The dream confirmed the castration anxiety he so assiduously avoided. Resistance prevented him from recognizing the dream's obvious representation of castration. I hoped to draw this to his attention without augmenting anxiety and hence more resistance. At the same time, I wanted to open the way for further associations or information, if not at the moment, then subsequently.

8
Aggression in the Dream

We have, so far, been concerned with dreams that lend themselves to interpretation on the basis of resistance, transference, and anxiety. We turn now to dreams that lend themselves to interpretation primarily on the basis of the drives associated with these phenomena.

In pregenital stages of development, differentiation between the sexual and aggressive drives is not yet complete. Therefore the dream as a vehicle of regression usually expresses sexuality and aggression in terms of one or the other, or both. Indeed, it is the commutability of the two drive representations that gives rise to problems in interpretation. Dreams and their associations enable us to elucidate the role each played in the past and is playing in the present.

The compelling significance of aggression in shaping man's destiny is no longer subject to dispute. Aggression as pure drive in the id, aggression that energizes ego defenses, and aggression that allies itself with archaic superego functioning, all require analytic evaluation. The interpretation of dreams helps expose the sources and derivatives of aggression and clarifies the nature of the ego's defenses against it. The dream work, as it is brought to bear on aggressive drive derivatives, roughly parallels, though it is not the equivalent of, the ego's mechanisms of defense. The dream work creates distortion by displacement and condensation or by obliteration of all traces of aggression. Analysis of the dream helps us identify and define the dream work's analogous counterparts in the ego's defensive system: projection, isolation, repression, and denial, which similarly try to deflect aggression from its course.

Dream interpretation traces the vicissitudes of aggression which contribute to the patient's pathology. The dream uncovers childhood fantasies in which aggressive drives (never free from their sexual component) are prominent. Aided by symbolic representation on a broad scale, the dream brings to the fore, in endless variety and complexity, aggressive drive derivatives from all developmental stages. The dream contains fantasies of drowning, flooding, penetrating, and consuming with fire which have their origin in the urethral and phallic stages, and fantasies of patricide and matricide from the oedipal phase. It pinpoints, at the oral level, fantasies of poisoning, biting, and devouring, and on the anal level, those of retention, soiling, and contamination. The interaction of sexual and aggressive impulses in the anal stage is responsible for the sadistic conception of the relations between the sexes, and constitutes the basis for such fantasies as rape, defecation as a sexual act, feces as a gift, and flatus as destructive and

144

persecutory. The fusion is also responsible for the mastur-batory character of beating fantasies.

Dreams not only reflect aggression that originates in the dreamer, they also play back the record of exposure to insult and injury actually sustained. Even as the dream portrays the analyst both as he is and as the patient conceives of him, so it presents evidence for aggression from both within and without. Hugo W.'s dream in which he felt pushed[1] was a response to what he thought an actual af-front. We cannot draw inferences from ostensibly aggres-sive images in the manifest dream without validation from associations and context.

The dream work transforms aggression both substan-tively and qualitatively, changing perpetrator into victim or innocent bystander, violence into tranquillity, venom into tenderness. Over and over the dream work camou-flages aggressive ideas and feelings behind a façade of bland benignity. The manifest dream of open assault, pursuit, or malicious attack can be totally misleading if accepted at face value; the latent content may harbor promptings of an entirely different nature. For example, passive homosexual urges often underlie the dream of assault by a person of the same sex. More broadly, love may exist under the defensive guise of hate. Once again we cannot afford to forget the distinction between manifest and latent content.

In clinical practice, our choice of interpretation is based on the context in which the dream is given. When we single out one element from among many, we select according to the relative weight and balance of the contents of the patient's mind, preconscious as against unconscious, past

[1] See dream, "Pushed parked car" (p. 71).

against present, defense against drive (erotic as against aggressive). We select for emphasis that which will have the most meaning for the patient at the moment.

While recognizing the admixture of sexual and aggressive drives in the latent content of the dreams in this section, I have here confined myself to those dreams whose associations and context called for interpretation of aggression, reserving the others for succeeding chapters.

Dinah B., an unmarried virgin in her late twenties, was deeply concerned over her lack of responsiveness to men and her failure to find a husband. Although she had quarreled with her slightly younger sister when they were children, the two had grown particularly intimate during the years before Dinah sought treatment (psychotherapy, in this case). Her sister entered treatment too, and a few months later the two girls left their parents' home to share their own apartment. Dinah prefaced the following dream by saying she had just heard that an old friend had died of leukemia.

> My sister had leukemia. We were all upset and worried, particularly my mother and I. What were we to do? Should we tell her? Then I had leukemia. I walked with a man but felt weak and tired and asked him to take me home early. Something about money.

She and her sister had quarreled with their father about money. . . . Although she had lost interest in sex lately, she wasn't particularly concerned about it. In the dream she was worried about her sister's illness and impending death but was not alarmed for herself. . . . She had a rectal itch that worried her. Perhaps she had cancer.

"Death is in the air—first your sister's, then your own—so morbid," I put in.

She found it strange to dream of her sister's death. This was at least the third time she remembered having done so. She felt guilty at having quarreled with her father; he had been awfully good to them.

"Your dream spoke of feeling bad about your sister. Now you speak of feeling responsible for unkindness to your father. Any connection?"

Well, her sister frequently asked her advice in conducting her love life, advice she was glad to offer.

"You are very good to her, especially when you have no love life of your own."

She knew her sister had long discussions with her psychiatrist concerning their involvement with each other.

"You don't mention her very often," I said.

Dinah elaborated on all she had done for her sister, how close they had been until recently, how alike they were in their problems with men. How could she wish her dead? They had even shared their earnings and kept a joint bank account. Hadn't there been something to do with money in the dream?

Dinah's almost homosexual bond with her sister was partly responsible for her failure to make a satisfactory heterosexual adjustment. She had heretofore clung strenuously to this reaction formation against her hostility. The dream brought the conflict into treatment (nonanalytic, hence my frequent interventions). I used it to draw attention to the hostility by questioning her defenses.

As we know, the child's ability to retain or expel his stool at will constitutes the basis for elaborate fantasies of power and destruction. Regression in the dream brings these fantasies and their aggressive content to the fore. The aggressive drive on the anal level of development assumes either active or passive forms (and frequently nothing is more aggressive than passivity) which influence all later aggressive manifestations.

For the most part, Paul D. kept his sadistic impulses on a fantasy level. He treated me with correct civility and rarely missed an appointment. One day he surprised me by arriving late, admitted he had dallied on the way, and, in a characteristic monotone, reported this dream:

> It was about shit. It was as if I were working in a big barn or factory. My job involved shoveling big balls of shit from some large animal, just to move the stuff around. Shoveling shit—I guess that's an old habit of mine. It seemed to be an assignment, specifically for menial work. It smelled. There were very large balls with an oblong shape.

Yesterday his boss, in a rage at somebody in the office, had used an expression containing the word, "shit."

A silence followed. I knew repressed aggression played a large part in Paul's pathology. The dream somehow struck me as incomplete and I wondered whether he had omitted anything. To break his silence and bring him back to the dream, I asked, "But nothing else happened in the dream?"

"No." He fidgeted silently for a time and then said he felt awfully tense. Last night he farted a lot and moved his bowels several times. Probably too much food and not enough exercise. The whole day seemed to have revolved around the subject of defecation. In bed he tried to withhold his farts to avoid offending his wife. He couldn't get to sleep, thinking about money and how much his wife spent. . . . Yesterday, in the midst of that row at the office, he found himself smiling and feeling elated that there was hell to pay. He wondered whether he was trying to shovel shit on any particular person. No, it didn't seem so, it was just general. Many years ago, when he was in the middle of a frustrating love affair, he first got the notion of eating shit. The phrase his boss had used, "Go shit in your hat," like the idea of eating shit, excited him. Being assigned work in the dream was like his job where he always had to take orders from above. Like working in a shit factory. . . . Maybe the dream referred to what he did with me; he seemed to spew out a lot of it here. He objected to people who did that and didn't like to think he did it. But he thought the dream was connected more with his boss than with me. The idea of having to go to the office made him tense. He wished he didn't have to be subordinate. If only he could be in charge, alone and uninterrupted.

Paul fell silent, and I noticed a marked increase in his restlessness. The fidgeting developed into jerking and thrashing about. When he added that he was glad his boss instead of himself was faced with problems, I said, "You can pile it on him, let him have the dirty part."

His squirming stopped and his mood brightened perceptibly. Almost exultantly (for him) he admitted that this was just what he had been doing, avoiding his responsibilities and letting someone else do it.

I did not accept Paul's denial of hostility toward me, especially in the light of his lateness that day. I left the object of rage on its displaced level because of the tentative expression of overt sadistic feelings and my knowledge of his

149

inability to face his sadism (unless its object was himself). I considered it sufficient to verbalize the wish around which his associations hovered so delicately.

Fantasy variations on themes taken from the anal stage have an individual style according to the nature and nurture of the child, even though the basic drives associated with this stage remain the same. The manifest content of dreams presented by two patients both contained reactive disgust to excrement. The dreams differed with reference to distortion, their position in the analysis, and the patients' diverse backgrounds and pathologies, but the latent content of both related to concern with money, anal withholding, and aggression carried over into the transference.

The first of these dreams came from George G. whose anal preoccupations and their derivatives, expressed in giving and withholding, invaded every one of his activities and relationships. He could find no accommodation between the two poles of his ambivalence. In the analysis, such defusion and sequestration posed a technical problem ever recurrent with this defense and made it necessary to pay special attention to the restoration of connections.

George began the hour by recapitulating a debate of parliamentary proportions he had been holding with himself ever since he had left his house: should he or should he not go to the bank? He decided not to, although he couldn't help feeling guilty for not having paid my bill. He had a dream to report:

> I needed to go to the bathroom to urinate. I found the toilet bowl filled with feces. It disgusted me. I wondered whether I should or should not flush the bowl. I didn't

know whether I should urinate in it without flushing it first. Would it overflow? I flushed it and it did overflow. I still needed to urinate.

He went on with further "shoulds" and "should-nots": he should have called his doctor but didn't; should he or should he not see his dentist about an aching tooth. . . . He advised a friend to see an analyst, telling him he should not see just anyone but should consult either of two people. . . . He trailed off into silence. I interrupted by asking him to repeat the dream. After he complied, I said, " 'Should or should not' was the first thing you said to me today."

He strained visibly in an effort to comprehend my meaning and finally recovered the memory of his opening remark, "Should I or shouldn't I go to the bank, should I or shouldn't I pay you." He talked without any real conviction of "dirty stuff" and "shit or get off the pot," then scampered off into platitudes. I nevertheless persisted, "I thought when I asked you about your dream and your first remark to me, you would see a connection: what you should and should not do here."

He remembered I had once mentioned his anal preoccupations, his putting things off. He spoke of feeling stuffed in my office, not talking, not giving, wanting to fart, to move his bowels when he was here. He reverted to his guilt at not paying me. He had thought of making me wait longer, just as he was making the other doctor wait for his phone call. Finally, I said, "You must have kept your mother waiting while you moved your bowels. You do the same thing here, as though you were on the toilet."

Even when patients verbalize a connection, they can remain unaware of it. I knew it was unwise to make an interpretation George could toy with, and tried to offer one

151

that would not get lost in an obsessional shuffle. I first suggested a connection, then spelled it out, and followed with a reconstruction. Of course, I did not proceed with the deliberation implied in this explanation. A few weeks later George alluded to the last intervention[2]—clear evidence it had reached him.

The second of the dreams belonged to Don J., whose many infantilisms and polymorphous perverse impulses were acted out on a grand scale. Oral and anal explosions incessantly threatened his equilibrium. To keep them under control was a major task both in and out of analysis. One day I told him my fee would be raised the next month. Neither then nor subsequently did he refer to this in any way, but the day after I presented him with a bill reflecting the increase, he brought a dream:

> I had moved to a new, larger apartment. While my girl was away I had another girl with me and had intercourse with her. After she left, I found a huge, disgusting bowel movement in the toilet. It was so tremendous I couldn't imagine a woman having had it. I kicked at the handle to flush the toilet but even so I got feces on my foot and hands. Then I was in a bed next to a window, like here in your office. People outside were looking in and making me furious.

His discursive associations alluded only warily to the dream. He mentioned wanting to move to a larger apartment and then drifted into a description of his latest sexual conquest. As usual after intercourse, he couldn't get rid of the girl fast enough. As usual too, he changed the sheets

[2] See dream, "Stuffed toilet on top floor" (p. 106).

right after she left. The sight of a bed in disarray after sex always filled him with disgust.

Don's lack of associations to the feces, so heavily accentuated in the dream, together with his complete silence regarding the raised fee, led me to say, "In the dream you kicked at an enormous amount of feces. Yesterday I presented you with an enormous bill."

He reacted as if shot. That had been on his mind all month. He hadn't been able to talk about it for fear I would be angry. He even had fantasies of fighting with me about it. Yet he had plenty of money, so why did he care so much? It made him think of how, the minute he saw any dirt or disorder in his apartment, he had to clean it up right away. He was reminded of having told me, at the beginning of analysis, of a temper tantrum he had as a child, how he got blue in the face and soiled himself.

Don's dream conveyed his suppressed grievance indirectly in regressive terms—as a bowel movement. My intervention supplied the connection. His dream had an expansive character (the bowel movement was "so tremendous") lacking in the dream of the far more constricted George.

In both instances the dream helped restore missing connections. In the first, I added a genetic reconstruction. Don, in a more advanced stage of treatment, with less ambivalence and less need to ward off aggressive impulses, required less help with the transference implications, and himself supplied a genetic association. The first dream was more concerned with ambivalence, the second with lack of control. Both dealt with aggression from similar developmental levels, largely the anal. Each required individual analytic emphasis according to the patient's character structure, psychic organization, ego state, and stage of analysis.

Some six months after Don J. deplored his "beastly" temper,[3] he was sufficiently troubled by recurrent attacks of nausea to consult a physician, whose findings were completely negative. The day after the consultation, he presented this dream:

> I was eating gobs of food. After a full rich meal I started to eat paper, cardboard, and stuff like that. I had to keep on eating even though I was stuffed—I just went on and on.

His stomach was turning when he awoke—he wanted to vomit. The nausea had persisted all day and was still with him.... Eating paper reminded him of a television commercial in which people took bites out of a hat.... He was bugged by his ambivalence to his girl friend. She loved him, she was good, but she bored him. Last night he met another girl and was hungry to undress her.

"Hungry?" I asked.

"Yes, I know, like the dream. Last night I had to avoid looking at the other dame I was so embarrassed by my thoughts."

He finished the evening with his own girl to whom he made love in his usual impersonal way, which included a good deal of biting. "I wanted to go down on her but I didn't."

"Eat her," I interposed.

He acknowledged his familiarity with the equivalence of

---

[3] See dream, "Monster squirts urine" (p. 139).

"going down," "eating," and cunnilingus and recalled several episodes of cunnilingus which he could practice only with women he didn't respect. Then he lapsed into a silence that lasted for the ten remaining minutes.

Don had been associating freely enough, but as is so often the case, did not see the relevance of his associations to his dream. We had already worked through many aspects of his destructiveness, his need to debase women. I knew that oral sadism contributed significantly to the complicated structure of his satyriasis. My earlier intervention was calculated to help him see connections without interfering with the flow of his ideas. The later interpretation was more explicit and was offered only when the repressed idea had become sufficiently preconscious for me to round it out.

Three months later, Don announced that he had to go away on business for a week. The prospect of getting rid of his "good" girl friend delighted him, and he had already arranged for sexual partners at his destination. He had a dream to tell me:

> I am in a concentration camp. All of us are men, many men. We are at the mercy of a woman who is going to kill us. She has fangs and will bite us in the neck. She is a shrike. We all try to avoid her by walking around in circles. It's just a question of time when I will be next.

His girl had made advances to him last night. He felt obliged to respond, though the more attention she showered on him, the less he wanted. Yet, even while he was rejecting her he felt guilty. "I feel as though I can be had by any woman."

"Turn that around," I said, "and the dream, too."

"I can't relate to anybody. I get rid of all my women after

a while. The more they tell me they care, the less I want to hear it." After a long pause, "Why do I always feel guilty when I'm going away?"

Another long silence. I did not want to disturb his dialogue with himself and forebore, as yet, telling him he had something to feel guilty about. Finally he said ruefully, "Last night I really treated her brutally."

Convinced that the link between his guilt and his rejection of the girl was sufficiently established, I said, "You are entitled to feel guilty. You know you consume women and then throw them away. You even arrange to have women waiting for you at the other end to pacify your guilt."

He expanded on his abominable treatment of his girl, adding, "Do you suppose what you just said has anything to do with my need to call my girl friends after they leave me, to say goodnight to them and make sure they got home safely?"

"Your question is a statement," I replied.

After almost a year of canceling appointments for what seemed to be pressing commitments elsewhere, Hugo W. became sufficiently caught up in the analysis to appear even when blizzards were raging. Once on the couch, he redressed the balance with intellectualizations and silences. Resistance, especially to any encounter with his aggressive impulses, was formidable, and made progress in this area almost imperceptible. He began one day by observing that it was curious how often, in his dreams, he felt that what he was dreaming was not possible, but then again, it was. As, for example, last night:

> I was listening to the radio when I heard the voice of an announcer say, "The United States has resigned from

the war in Vietnam." I couldn't believe I had heard it right. It couldn't be possible and yet it seemed the news was indeed true, however unlikely it sounded.

He had the odd feeling that he had dreamed the same thing twice in succession. The content in both dreams was the same except that the first time, the voice came from the radio, the second time, from the television set. Before the dream, he had been mad as hops at his wife. They had dinner with another couple, and she complained so insufferably throughout the meal, he could hardly endure it. He'd been putting up with her shrewishness for ten years, but last night he was so furious he found himself clenching his fists. On the way home he couldn't bear to talk to her, kept a distance between them, and fumed to himself, "How is it possible I have tolerated this for so long? It simply can't be."

"Have you any ideas about 'resigning from the war'?" I asked.

He thought it referred to his resignation in a double sense: to be resigned to or to resign from marriage.

Hugo's dream expressed the ambivalence to be expected from obsessional character disorders. Both the manifest dream and the associations clearly reflected an obsessional need for doing and undoing (it is possible—it isn't). The intellectual temper of his associations precluded my making an explicit interpretation. Nevertheless, the pressure of reality had overcome his powers of denial, if only momentarily, and the associations to his dream said so.

Six months later Hugo reverted to the same subject. During one of his more productive hours, he paused long enough in his flight from himself to acknowledge more freely the sadomasochistic nature of his marriage. He said he was beginning to realize he had been playing ostrich for years, struggling to maintain a harmonious façade when he was in fact only too aware of his wife's objectionable qualities.

"Why does this happen to you?" I asked.

He elaborated, recalling the number of times she had humiliated him even before they were married. He wondered why he always refused to see the obvious. What was he afraid of?

The following day, Hugo surprised me by saying he had left the previous session with the greatest reluctance; he had even had an impulse to turn back •nd knock at my door so he could go on with it. His statement was so at variance with his customary reserve that I felt safe in assuming he had accepted my intervention as coming from an ally. Then he told me this dream:

> I was walking with a friend. We came to a butcher shop. Here the friend left me. I saw the butcher inside. He was blind. The shop was in shadow, brown-colored. The butcher called my name in a down-east Boston accent. I wanted meat for my cat. Though blind, he cut up a kidney with a sharp knife.

He thought the butcher whom he blinded was me.

"What makes you think so? What about the 'down-east' accent?"

"Well, that does sound more like the way I talk," he conceded.

"You said you had wanted to go on yesterday with the problem of your defective vision."

He was reminded of a man whose ideas he could never understand although they were clear enough to everyone else. He could never see them. And he never seemed to hear anything the first time, either. "No see, no hear, no know; that's me." He recalled a detail of the dream: there had been no door to the shop. It was wide open to enter if he wanted.

"Why must I be so blind?" he asked.

"Why the butcher?" I replied.

"The man who chops everything up so it's butchered."

"There is something you don't want to look at ..." I started, but he interrupted, "The butcher had an accent like an actor whose name is Kil[l]bride," adding, after a momentary pause, "what do you know!"

The dream had taken up the theme of the previous hour and announced a new development in his struggle against denial: "No door to the shop," he could "enter if he wanted." Analysis of resistance and defenses had permitted him to face his homicidal rage, even if gingerly, in a dream.

Jenny K.'s attitude toward her mother was classic in its ambivalence. When mother went away, Jenny missed her; within hours of a reunion, the two were at each other's throats. The following dream antedates Jenny's dreams given in previous sections.

I walked in the country and saw a woman driving a car. She drove so carelessly that another car couldn't avoid her and crumpled her fender. It knocked off her hat. As it fell to the ground I saw it had a goosefeather on it.

Yesterday she had met her mother to go shopping. It had been awful. Mother's hauteur and condescension had reduced the poor salesman to a state of groveling servility. She

THE DREAM IN CLINICAL PRACTICE

herself always had such trouble finding the right tone to adopt to salespeople. . . . Mother might be old-fashioned in her ideas, but she certainly knew how to get what she wanted.

"So she's a goose whose head you could take off," I said.

A startled silence—as though she had been caught off guard—then, haltingly, "She does so much for me, wants to buy me clothes, wants me to look soignée the way she does, but I can't stand her telling me what to do. . . . Always asking why don't I get married, why don't I do this, do that. I suppose she's interested enough, but it drives me up the wall. . . . She's such a hypocrite. She knows she's better-looking than I am and then she asks father, 'Isn't she pretty?' and he says, 'uh, huh,' as if he didn't know who she was talking about and couldn't care less.. . .."

Jenny spent the rest of the hour elaborating on her resentment of women, especially those who were chic and attractive to men. Although still a long way from integrating her hostility toward women with her feelings for her mother, she had declared herself more freely than heretofore, making especially clear to me her identification with her mother, who "knew how to get what she wanted."

Antipathy for his father kept Simon E. in constant turmoil. He found it impossible to control his temper when with him and, for the rest, gave rein to incessant fantasies which had his father's death and the disposition of his estate as their invariable central theme. The fantasies varied only in their ending: his father either cut him off without a cent, leaving his entire fortune to Simon's brother, or, repentant, left it all to him. At one juncture, Simon imagined himself particularly desperate for money and invoked the second version of his fantasy. Acting on impulse, he made an ingratiating phone call to his father, who offered his appreciation for the show of warmth, but nothing more. That night he dreamed:

> I was walking amiably with my father in a garden. He asked me a question about some flowers. I flared up, shouting, "What a stupid question!" He looked at me amazed and in turn upbraided me. I got more and more furious and would have struck him.

In tones which grew progressively lower until they were barely audible, he consumed the greater part of the hour talking about people who were better off than he, of domestic problems, and of his difficulties in meeting his obligations. Then, as if changing the subject and in passing, he mentioned a question I had put to him the day before. The dream flashed into mind and made me say, " 'What a stupid question!' "

"Well," he said, "it seemed to me you weren't paying attention or you wouldn't have had to ask me that question."

He followed this with a storm of abuse, raging at me, his family, and the world at large. Then he exhaled deeply and said, "I feel tons lighter now."

You may ask why I did not choose to stress the obvious and connect the dream with his fight with his father. Again, I was guided by his associations. After a repetition of grievances with which we were both thoroughly familiar, he referred offhandedly to my stupid question. My intervention, quoting the dream, gave Simon an opportunity to see the connection between myself and his father if he would. We both frustrated him by our "stupidity" and indifference. His hostility to his father was conscious (as well as unconscious) and could be justified. The parallel hostile current to me was harder for him to justify. Resolution of his conflict would be found only in the transference. "What a stupid question" was the bridge. The sexual connotation of "garden" and "flowers" suggested that the argument with his father had as much to do with sexuality as with money. Absence of pertinent associations precluded further investigation of this aspect of the dream. Nor did I interpret the contribution of his superego. "What a stupid question" referred to the question he did not ask his father: "How much money will I get?" More important for the time being was the dream's revelation of a latent reaction to me which might otherwise have gone undetected.

A few weeks later Simon brought this dream:

> I am a child playing in the ocean where the waves break. My father is standing over me, smiling, playing with me, but he is holding my head under water. I can't breathe and get frightened. I struggle to catch my breath, feel frantic, helpless, angry. I take a chance and breathe in, although I'm not sure my head is out of water. To my relief I breathe in air.

His associations revolved around his proverbial hostility toward his father. When he said, "Last night I was thinking about him and got so mad I found myself about to say out loud, 'Goddam him!' ", I said, "In a breath-holding temper tantrum you would eventually have to stop and take a breath."

His voice rose dramatically, "I remember crying with rage when I didn't get what I wanted. I was a spoiled brat, no question about it. Nobody could make me stop; I couldn't stop myself until I finally took a deep breath. Now I seem to have to hold myself back from doing the same thing with my own family."

162

Neither historical evidence nor his associations indicated that the dream scene duplicated an actual childhood experience. I chose to make a reconstruction because of the specific dream representation of breath-holding within the framework of Simon's current analytic position. We do not always get such buoying confirmation of our reconstructions even when they are accurate. Days, weeks, or months may elapse before we find out whether or not we were right.

Working through his aggression had made it increasingly ego-alien and had revived, in a dream, an infantile drive expression and ego state. The breath-holding could be seen as an equivalent for stool retention, an additional sign of the developmental level from which the dream arose. On a deeper level, immersion in water hinted at birth, specifically—because of the father-analyst figure represented—rebirth. Several days later Simon dreamed of a friend who described to him how he was starting all over again in a professional venture. Simon's associations indicated his own wish to be reborn, to be a different person, and do things differently the second time around. The reference to analysis was transparent and constituted an elaboration of the earlier dream.

Thinking himself a model of benevolence and high-mindedness, John Y. liked to boast of his willingness to defer to others and his ability to remain composed under the severest provocation. He had no trouble squaring this self-image with his habit of disparaging almost everyone who came within his ambit. Efforts to confront him with the disparity produced intellectual acceptance but little conviction. John continued to dismiss his critical judgments as mere thoughts and therefore of no particular significance or relevance. In the course of an hour filled with complaints that nothing was happening either in or outside analysis, he remembered a dream:

> I was in a room with a man who lay on a bed. He was sick or very tired. He turned over on his face and seemed to want to sleep. I covered him tenderly to keep him warm and help him get to sleep.

He had been taking care of his girl friend who was sick. She had accused him of being entirely too solicitous about her mild indisposition and made him feel like a hypocrite. . . . In a way, the man on the bed made him think of the way he behaved here with me. . . . He had recently taken to reading obituary notices. . . . He had been thinking of how hard I worked, thought I looked tired, and wondered whether I ever got any rest. He had just heard of a doctor who died of a heart attack. He was well aware of his need to disclaim his hostile impulses; I had made that sufficiently clear to him, but why the dream and who was the man?

"You want to put me to sleep permanently, not tenderly," I said.

"Why am I always so agreeable?" he answered with a rueful chuckle, as though we were having a social conversation.

My interpretation restated a hostile impulse that was known but not felt. His response was as much as I could have expected for the time being. Certainly he showed no sign of readiness to accept the oedipal implications which existed at a much deeper level and were evident in the dream.

A few weeks later, when I crossed the room to get something from my desk, he told me he had an impulse to kick me. I said, "That, too, is a form of relationship and contact." Aggression has its uses after all.

John's resistance in analysis went hand in hand with an acting out of his fantasies elsewhere. His behavior pattern was unconsciously designed as a counterphobic defense against the warnings of his superego and was well calculated to arouse retaliatory superego reactions. John had this dream after a friend told him his contumacy and recklessness were bringing his job into jeopardy.

> I am with my sister walking up a rocky, bare hill. A war seems to be developing. Enemy tanks are confronting each other, circling around as if something is about to start. I seem to be getting into it. There is an American tank which reassures me, like a protection.

Several people had warned him against going along with a chap at the office who was planning to play a practical joke on the top brass. He knew he was playing with fire, but the idea tickled him so much he was strongly tempted anyway.... He actually loved to play with fire when he was a kid. His sister recently told him he had once almost set their house on fire.

I understood the dream as a wish for protection against hostile impulses cloaked under the guise of horseplay and said, "You are still playing with fire and you are trying to get me to tell you to stop."

His first wife used to tell him he ought to set limits on himself, but he did admire people who took things into their own hands and charged ahead. "When I was a kid, the minute my parents left the house, I thought of all the forbidden things I could do. As for that American tank, it was there for my protection. I guess I *am* telling you this in the hope that you'll tell me to stop."

9
The Dream and Infantile Sexuality

Unconscious infantile fantasies are as invisible as the instinctual drives they represent, every bit as influential and persistent. Together with their developmental sources, they may be inferred from a patient's character, symptoms, and behavior; but nothing matches the dream in providing almost graphic evidence of their existence. After all, the sexual drives and their derivatives, as well as those of aggression, constitute the very mainspring for the creation of the dream. It is therefore hardly surprising that the dream has a uniquely hypermnestic capacity and access to these fantasies of early life.

The dream focuses attention, both ours and the patient's, on sexual experiences otherwise buried in the rubble of childhood and infancy. It is the chief means by which we can recover not only the fantasies but the ego states, including anxiety, originally associated with them. Even representations of libidinal excitation stemming from pre-verbal levels find their way into dreams, usually in the form of somatic memories or perceptions which may be tactile, visual, auditory, olfactory, and occasionally gustatory.

Sometimes the dream makes it possible for us to recon-struct these early fantasies. Sometimes they appear in the manifest content, disguised it is true, but nevertheless plain to see if we utilize our knowledge of symbolization, symbols being the guise under which they frequently make their appearance. The manifest dream is, however, by no means an accurate indicator of the prevalence or relative prepon-derance of either sexual or aggressive instinctual drives in the latent thoughts. Censorship and distortion may produce a disarmingly innocuous manifest dream. Or, because of the commutability of the two drives, the erotic manifest dream may mask aggression in the latent thoughts, and aggression in the manifest dream may lead to distinctly erotic latent contents.

Instant recognition of a sexual drive representation in a dream can tempt us to premature interpretation. Analytic procedure demands, however, that we accord first place to an estimation of the patient's ego state, the character of the therapeutic alliance, the context, and associations, all sub-sumed under the heading of analytic tact. Optimally, interpretation should seek a point of accommodation which links these early sexual experiences with current reality.

Throughout his career, Simon E. had relied on the ful-fillment of the secret wish that someday, somehow, he would succeed to the throne, be proclaimed conquering hero, winner of the fair lady's hand, and possessor of boundless wealth. The need to relinquish infantile fantasies and attachments resulted in a period of prolonged mourning. In this atmosphere of disappointment, deprivation, and depression, he brought a dream containing a repressed fantasy.

> I was in an apartment with a colored girl. We were going to have an affair. It was as if the affair existed but also didn't. I knew she would offer to take my penis in her mouth and the thought excited me. In the dream it seemed it happened, and yet I knew it didn't.

He spoke of his general feeling of apathy, indifference, and frustration. Nothing interested him, neither family, work, friends, nor the world at large.

Simon did not refer to the dream, but as he talked his manner clearly conveyed narcissistic preoccupation and withdrawal of libido. I correlated this with the dream image of fellatio, reading the colored girl as a less inhibited aspect of himself.

"You must have thought of taking your penis in your own mouth," I said.

He instantly recalled having tried to do just that when he was adolescent. He was astounded to think he could have put it so completely out of his mind for more than twenty years. He also remembered that shortly after forcing himself to abandon the idea, he had entertained the odd notion that what he had done was not real but only a dream ("the affair existed but also didn't ... it happened, and yet I knew it didn't").

The context of the dream made it possible to offer a reconstruction. The frustration attendant on working through the weaning process had thrown Simon back onto an earlier source of satisfaction, himself. I knew he had been a persistent thumb-sucker. The fantasy of autofellatio followed this antecedent model to console him in the current circumstances; its occurrence in the dream served the general function of fantasy as substitute for implacable and unpalatable reality.

Some six months later, following a relaxed weekend with his family, Simon reported a dream which introduced another infantile fantasy.

> I walked down a flight of stairs into a white-tiled finished basement. It was full of water. Looking to see where the water was coming from, I noticed an old nurse from my childhood standing by an icebox. She seemed to be trying to stop a leak but couldn't. I tried to find the leak to shut it off.

There had been pools of water on his kitchen floor yesterday. His children and their friends had been in and out of the house all weekend. Two of them had taken a bath together.... His wife told him one of their neighbors was pregnant. He certainly enjoyed his children, especially the younger boy who was a charmer....

Simon's dream with its typical symbols ("walking down the stairs, going into a basement full of water"), together with the associations that followed, revealed the trend of his latent thoughts. When he spoke of his youngest child, I said, "You might have thought of having more children, but also felt you had to put a 'stop' to it."

"Huh! My wife was just asking me if I didn't want another! Of course I like being the proud papa, but it makes me shudder at the same time. I'd like a dozen, but how can I? First there's the money. And I remember when the nurse left after the last one, I felt so helpless, didn't know what to do. I wouldn't want to go through that again. Sure, I love having kids around when I'm not hating them for getting in my way."

"You'd like to be the proud papa," I said, "but you'd also like to be the child."

I understood the "old nurse" as a reference to his own infancy. Taken together with the symbolism of entering or emerging from water, the dream condensed the wish for his own rebirth with that of wanting more children. Simon's interest in his younger boy stemmed from identification with him—he too was a younger son.

When Paul D. started analysis, he displayed such difficulty in expressing himself, I thought he suffered from a speech or perhaps even a thinking disorder. I revised my impression upon discovering that his inarticulateness was restricted to the analytic sessions. His friends thought him a little on the quiet side, nothing more. Still later, I learned that when he was a child he had been far more silent at home than in school or elsewhere. As analysis progressed, Paul improved markedly in this respect until he was, on the whole, speaking with normal freedom.

A few days after I returned from a week's vacation to which he had made absolutely no reference, he began an hour with a prolonged silence, reminiscent of his early taciturnity. Finally he said he had a dream to report.

> I was dead. I knew I was dead, but I knew I was still alive. I couldn't talk to anybody, communicate with anyone.

He said he had never dreamed anything like this. He felt dead and behaved that way too. As a matter of fact, he was the only deadhead in his family. His father and brothers were lively and his mother had been positively vivacious until she began to fail. . . .

Speaking even more listlessly than usual, Paul continued:

171

during the weekend he tried to comfort his wife who was disappointed because her parents could not visit them as planned. When she left the house for a few hours, he grew restless and masturbated, feeling like a child whose mother had left him alone.

The dream's emphasis on communication, together with his silence, particularly with respect to my vacation, and the loneliness hinted at in his associations prompted me to intervene.

"Your mother is dead and you have no one to talk to, no one who would know how you felt without your having to say anything."

His response was electric, if of low voltage. For the rest of the hour he talked with rare animation. He had indeed been thinking of his mother, of the complete understanding that had existed between them. A glance exchanged had been sufficient. ... How little he found to say to people, even to his wife. Now as he thought of the dream, if he were dead he would be joined to his mother and there would be no need for talk (here I inserted a corroboratory "yes"). He had been depressed while I was away, had wanted to talk to me, and yet resented his dependence on me. How difficult it was for him to communicate with anyone; how well his mother must have understood him to have been able to meet his needs without his having to say a word.

Throughout the analysis, nothing had made the source of Paul's communication difficulty as clear as this dream and its associations. The symbolic connection between silence and death helped me understand what was going on.

Paul was distressed not so much by his need to masturbate as by the persistence of sadomasochistic beating fantasies which were a necessary accompaniment to masturbation if he was to achieve orgasm. Analysis never quite succeeded in resolving this aspect of his pathology, although it enabled him to obtain considerable heterosexual gratification. We had already worked through many instances of the acting out in derivative form of his beating fantasies, and he already had a nodding acquaintance with his unconscious infantile fixation linking sex and sadism when he brought the following dream.

> I was at a party. The people there were all relatives. I began to realize they were talking about having to kill my baby. Then I knew they meant I had to kill her.

He puzzled over the dream for a while, without seeming unduly affected by it. He spoke of the pleasure he got from playing with his little girl, of her gaiety and responsiveness (I was so accustomed to him in his role of prophet of doom and gloom, I was surprised to hear that anything gave him pleasure). More hesitantly and almost inaudibly, he admitted that he became sexually excited when fondling her.

To re-establish the connection which he, in typically obsessional fashion, undid, I said, "In the dream you killed your daughter. Yet you have sexual feelings for her. Who would think there was any connection, that they go together?"

He told me that yesterday he masturbated and again had one of his old beating fantasies. He went on to recall innumerable occasions when he sought out painful experiences and derived a curious satisfaction from them. Sexual excitement from torture and hating seemed so crazy, so incomprehensible.

My intervention was merely a variation on an old theme.

173

The dream permitted me to show him a new version of the problem. By putting this new version into words, I relieved his anxiety as attested to by his subsequent associations.

The very next day Paul presented another dream. This was somewhat out of character: I had come to consider one dream a week profusion for him.

> It was here with you. We sat facing each other, man to man. You were telling me about your problems, not sexual, but about school or teaching. I was listening and wanted to comfort you.

As I listened, several ideas flashed into mind: "man to man" suggested a homosexual wish; sitting face to face precluded free association, made the situation more social than professional, and raised the possibility of resistance. I knew that when he was younger, his father had come to him with family problems and he had acted as arbiter. His listening to "my problems," his show of concern for me, certainly gave the appearance of a reaction formation, the defensive reversal of hostility. I shook off these thoughts, reminding myself they were mine, not his. In following the manifest dream too literally I was violating the basic rule that the manifest dream must not be taken at face value and is but the starting point for associations.

Paul had just been visited by his father who gave him some money. While grateful, he felt obligated and dependent, just as he did here with me. My superiority, my having the advantage over him made him feel helpless, as if I were beating him down.... His beating fantasies made him feel childish too. At home he acted like an autocrat, was impatient with his wife, and wanted her to wait on him the way his mother used to.

I did not intervene. Like so many dreams, this one could have been interpreted on a variety of levels. Viewed one way, relief stands out as the central motif. The problem was "not sexual," not the horrid, fascinating, sadomasochistic fantasies, and what's more, did not even belong to him. The dream could have represented a fulfillment of a wish to escape from his objectionable impulses. Or we could as readily conclude that the dream expressed hostile intentions. His father gives and he resents; I give and he resents. The reversal of roles contains the wish to humiliate me in retaliation for my help. The comforting aspect is the opposite of beating. Just as he "beat" his wife with his lordly demands (and screened these with solicitude for her), so his concern for me in the dream concealed feelings of hostility. Or perhaps the dream was a reaction to the previous hour and expressed resistance: let's not go into the dirty unconscious with its sex, sadism, and all that. In retrospect, I think the last-mentioned was most applicable. Because I was not sure at the time, I said nothing.

The reserved and impeccably correct Hugo W. did not bring many dreams, and when he did, they were either vague or lacked associations. With Hugo I had to learn to live with ambiguity, and nowhere more so than in his dreams. Those that follow were far from clear, but seemed to offer some access, however limited, to his unconscious.

Shaving or washing at a sink, not in my own house— a hotel, resort, or rented place. The shaving or washing took a long time. A bath was running at the same time. I wasn't looking and didn't notice it was overflowing until water rose under the sink. I thought, "Oh my! It's going to go through the ceiling and cause hell! How terrible! I could mop it up." I did mop it up and returned to shaving. The same thing seemed to happen again. Water all over, deep. I reached down into the bathtub. Why wasn't it draining? I reached down to free something that wasn't open. My arm got wet. Then I knew I had solved the problem.

He had trouble falling asleep last night, brooding over the antagonism between his mother and his wife. Although they both knew he liked to keep things smooth, they put him under a terrible strain by refusing to talk to each other. He felt caught between them.

"In your dream you were caught between the bath and the sink," I interposed.

Yes, and the drain wasn't working—like his penis. He had approached his wife yesterday morning but she wasn't penetrable.

"Wasn't open," I added.

He agreed—like the valve he was trying to open in the dream. Trying to get to sleep last night he felt his penis and testicles dangling and "reached down with his hand" (I said nothing). Everybody was denying everybody else in his family. He denied his wife and his mother; they both denied him and each other.... Last night he thought of masturbating.

Referring to the fact that his hour was almost over, I said, "You got that in just under the wire. In the dream you got your arm wet. And masturbation is at least one satisfaction you can provide for yourself."

In view of my limited understanding of the dream, I confined myself to making whatever connections I could between it and his associations. Had he not mentioned masturbation, I would not have made my final observation.

Perhaps I was on the right track, for the next day he started by reporting another dream.

> About fishing. I was going upstate to fish. I had built a house there to go to. It had no windows. But strangely enough it was far away from the fishing area, some sixty or so miles away.

He'd had an awful row with his wife because he wanted to go off fishing for a weekend and she hated fishing. He said to her, "I'm not your whipping post, I'm not your scapegoat, I'm not your anything!" She seized on the last word and accused him of keeping himself apart from her. Afterwards, he couldn't get to sleep so he took a drink and masturbated.

"And then you had the dream?"

"That's right. The house without windows where nobody can see what I'm doing, where I'm alone."

"When you masturbate you don't need anybody else."

Hugo described his increasing sense of alienation from his wife and, lately, from his child. Then he digressed into a review of what had been going on at his office but interrupted himself to observe, "Again I keep myself away from you and all to myself."[1]

The associations all unfolded to the same point: his removal of himself from intimate contact with people. I will only add that he was working through the secondary narcissistic basis for his pathology more meaningfully than before. The dreams and what preceded them reflected his attempts to make good the deficiency of mothering by mothering himself.

[1] See dream, "Men dancing with men" (p. 112), which took place two weeks earlier.

Notwithstanding persistent character analysis, George G.'s transference reactions pursued their course on a pregenital level and his fantasies followed suit. Sex was inextricably linked with the toilet, masturbation preferable to intercourse, and other people's sexual activities (especially mine) more interesting than his own. The nature of his fantasies and the ease, almost eagerness, with which he revealed those involving myself, would have caused me to suspect more severe pathology had I not known that outside analysis George adapted quite adequately. I put this tone of the transference atmosphere down to his childhood experiences with his mother with whom he must have shared and acted out who knows what. When his most intimate thoughts, once expressed, led nowhere, he repeated them as if mere verbiage would substitute for analytic work. I finally suggested that a great deal of what he said told him nothing he did not already know. The next day, grumbling that he felt more irritable than usual, he began with this dream:

> A woman was talking to an audience in a large room. The people there seemed to know what she had to say. She became irritable. Then I was walking with her through some rooms in a hospital. We lay down together on an operating table. It felt good to have my arms around her. I started to have an orgasm and tried to hold it back with my hand. Then something about two beds, a toilet bowl, and using a sink to urinate in.

I knew at once the woman represented the female aspect of himself ("she became irritable.... The people ... seemed to know what she had to say"). George's associations corroborated my assumption.

He had not wanted to have intercourse last night when his wife approached him; he thought of me as he refused her. ... The operating table reminded him of the couch; the woman talking sounded like himself, here. Lying together with her made him think again of lying on my couch.

"It feels good to lie there on the couch with yourself." I deliberately left my intervention open-ended to avoid a confrontation that would sound judgmental or condemnatory.

"Yes, that's just what I was thinking," he answered, "and now I'm beginning to feel very uncomfortable."

He had thought of masturbating last night. Now he was beginning to feel sexually excited. The thought of touching himself excited him. Perhaps I would touch him. He wanted more from me; I hadn't gone far enough. It seemed the dream was about masturbating himself here, using himself for himself.

I said as much as I thought advisable in light of his passivity. I had demonstrated the dream's reference to a masturbation fantasy in which he played the roles of male and female. I did not want to overwhelm him by saying that the fantasy was a reaction to the frustration of his homosexual wishes in the transference.

The anxiety evoked by Jenny K.'s masturbatory activities and her reluctance to discuss them have already been mentioned.[2] She brought this dream when resistance to the subject was just beginning to emerge.

I went riding in the park. The horse began to canter.
I was holding the reins with one hand and felt the horse
was getting out of control. He took a path which finally

[2] See Chapters 5 and 7, sessions referring to dreams, "Love in a pastoral setting" (p. 89) and "Misses appointment, can't dial analyst" (p. 132).

forced him to slow down. Back at the stable, I found a
man instructing a boy to hold the reins with both hands.
I felt I would now know what to do, and as though I had
discovered a new game to play.

She remembered her pleasure in riding when she was
younger, and the opportunities life in the country provided
for observing animals' sexual activity. Her mother had
never been able to countenance the idea of sex, even among
bees, and still registered shock when she saw her grandsons
handling themselves.... Yesterday she held a friend's
daughter on her lap and was amused when the child un-
selfconsciously put her hand in her own vagina.

"In your dream you discovered a game you could play
with your hands," I said.

Jenny's voice took on a new guardedness as she treated
me to an academic dissertation on comparative anatomy of
the male and female genitalia, finally breaking off to say
she had an urgent need to urinate.

The dream and associations suggested a recent recurrence
of either masturbation or masturbation fantasies. Jenny
could be sexually broad-minded until I approached the
deeper implications of her masturbation. Then she took on
a sudden resemblance to her mother and projected her
disapproval onto me.

A few weeks later Jenny had a dream which threw light
on what lay behind her passionate, though not compassionate, interest in men:

I was walking with a man dressed in a naval uniform.
A little girl appeared and sidled up to him. He wanted to
give her his coat, but I didn't let him. I wanted him to
give it to me.

One of the men at her office had been making a play for another girl, and though the man meant nothing to her, she couldn't help feeling jealous.... The previous evening, while waiting for a call from a man she planned to conquer, she filled the time with erotic reveries.... She had heard of a book which described circumcision as the removal of a sleeve from a coat, and this made her think of a penis.

In view of Jenny's pathology, her last association, and the "coat" in the manifest dream, I said, "A coat is dream code for a penis."

"In my dream, imagine!" she replied.... She often felt that women married in order to be made complete and to acquire something they lacked, but she was sure she had never thought of this in explicitly anatomical terms.... She had to admit that, when she masturbated, she imagined herself playing both roles but was always brought up short by the intrusion of the thought, "What do I do for a penis?".... She recalled little girls' asking each other which they'd rather do, menstruate or shave. The boys always seemed to get the best of everything.

"You must have felt it was unfair that boys appeared so much better off and that you had to race to keep up with them."

"Damn!" her voice rose, "My brother ... thought he knew it all ... invited me to watch him pee—I must have been about five—and said, 'Now let's see you do it.' I remember saying, 'What do I need it for anyway?' But I fled, ashamed, angry, excited, all mixed up, and thinking, 'Someday, someday.' Someday what? It still seems that way."

Women's dreams motivated predominantly by penis envy always include an aggressive element—rage in reaction to deprivation. Men's dreams of phallic striving, however, in addition to their quota of aggression, are attended by fear of retaliatory castration. The possessors of the penis must suffer the fate of all possessors—anxiety lest what they have be taken away. The deprived can only bemoan their deficiency. A loss is always harder to sustain than a lack.

By exercising enormous self-control, Jenny temporarily stopped acting out in sexual promiscuity, but complained that abstinence was making her feel lonely, frustrated, and withered. Then she had this dream:

> I was in a grocery store in the country. There were three rooms, a sort of living room and two back rooms. I went in and found it was self-service in a still smaller room at the back where meat was cut. That was all.

The symbolism here could hardly be ignored. I read the "store" as analysis, the "rooms" as female anatomy, and "self-service" with "meat" being "cut" as a rebus for masturbation and castration. Her associations rounded out the dream's symbolic shorthand.

The "store" made her think of analysis. Last night she had been brooding over her lack of a sex life. She had met a man who seemed interested, but he didn't strike her as any more masculine than all the other men she found disappointing. She had nevertheless allowed herself a few fantasies. . . . She remembered how often she was frigid . . . wished she hadn't discussed these things with her girl friends. . . . The man she'd been thinking of had a beard, which made her think with distaste of the female genitalia. And, oh yes, now she remembered she had another dream last night.

> A cat was doing something obscene with meat. It was sitting on it and made me think of the vagina.

182

Jenny's reference to her distaste for the female genitalia had reminded her of the second dream and could therefore be considered an association to it. In view of the second dream's almost explicit reference to masturbation, the absence of this subject from her associations was all the more significant.

"But nothing happened," I said.

"You mean nothing happened last night. No, it didn't. I didn't masturbate but I sure wanted to. Only having to come and tell you about it prevented me."

My intervention was designed to indicate that I understood her efforts to control her impulse. It is important that we convey to patients not only our comprehension, but our ability to appreciate what they are experiencing. Instead of acting out, Jenny had a dream that brought the problem of masturbation into analysis where it could be dealt with. Her allusions to analysis and genitalia made clear the final "that was all" of the first dream—"that's all there is to it, I didn't do anything."

One day Jenny, looking like a thundercloud, launched into an indictment of me and analysis in general. She accused me of smugness, of minimizing her distress, claimed to be feeling worse instead of better, and threatened to leave treatment. Her outburst caught me by surprise. My recollection of her previous hour provided no clues. She brushed aside my request for information that might account for her tirade and redoubled her scorn for my feeble therapeutic efforts. On this note, the hour came to an end. The next day, still looking grim, she began with a dream:

I was with the President of the United States. He gave me a fountain pen, one he had just used to sign a document of some sort.

She told of a recent visit to her gynecologist. He had examined her thoroughly, shrugged off the concern she voiced over the irregularity of her periods, and dismissed her with a clean bill of health. Strangely enough, she had trouble remembering when her periods were due and was always unprepared for them. It had been five weeks since her last one, and she hoped she wasn't pregnant.

With the previous hour and the current dream in mind, I said, "How much better it would be if you had no need to worry about your periods."

A torrent of tears was followed by a flood of associations. It wasn't fair that women had to have so much trouble with menstruation. She was never normal. She felt damaged, defective, wanted her period but at the same time dreaded it (Here she interjected, "Now I suddenly feel much less resentful of you than when I walked in."). She had been angry with me because the treatment didn't seem to be helping. She had wanted to punish me, had thought, "Why should I talk? I have nothing to talk about."[3] Perhaps the delayed period had something to do with her mood. But the whole subject of menstruation struck her as so banal she hated to mention it. As a man, I could never understand how she felt about that! "Men with their masculine mystique, their superior ways, their dominance!"

The dream expressed in symbolic form her wish for a penis, and she had "nothing to talk about." The question was, why the dream at that particular time and how to make use of it. Her associations provided the answers.

---

[3] See dream, "Love in a pastoral setting" (p. 89), which occurred a week after the hour under discussion here.

After approximately a year of face-to-face psychotherapy twice a week, Dinah B. entered regular analysis. During the preparatory period, she lived first with her mother, then with her sister, and finally by herself. Her social life also took on a fresh dimension. For the first time since her early teens, she had a young man in attendance. True, he was not her ideal and his presence on the scene raised serious questions. He was too passive, too compliant. His sexual overtures repelled her. But if she sent him packing, she would be left utterly alone, a condition she could not contemplate.

For a month or more, her analytic sessions revolved around the problem of her suitor and the adjustment to the change in treatment. I had prepared her carefully. We had discussed both the advantages of analysis and what it entailed. She nevertheless found the new arrangement far from satisfactory. I didn't say enough, do enough. I was too cold and distant. Her friends in analysis seemed much more involved with their analysts than she was. Once, when she faulted me for my aloofness after describing how she rejected her young man, I observed that she might conceivably be doing the same thing with me. (The reality factor attributable to the changeover was understandable; her interpretation of it was another matter.) This dream followed.

It was a very strange dream. I was alone in a small room. Yigael Yadin, the archaeologist, suddenly comes in and tells me he has to dig through my apartment, fix the pipes, take down a connecting wall. I have a feeling I'm married to him. Then he dies and I'm left alone. I am walking down a hallway and see a scene like on TV; dancing cigarettes and cardboard cigarette boxes. It's a free place for everybody to go to bed together. Couples are in rooms having intercourse, one couple doing it in the bathroom. I am in a kimono and want a cigarette but it's Saturday, Sabbath, and it's not nice. I can't. Also I have no match. Then I felt it was all not me. It was about somebody else. My husband wasn't dead, the woman was Madame X, a famous character in Israel.

Even as she told the dream, she felt she was just an observer, not a participant. There were so many things she couldn't do for religious reasons.... She was doing a study of Sholem Aleichim who wrote about love, marriage, the relations between people. In the dream, talking to Yadin, again she felt like an observer, "It was me and yet not me."

"Just as you feel in this room with me," I said.

She agreed she felt like an observer with me and wished she could participate more. That's what she had been complaining about. When she talked to her friends about treatment, they told her they felt so involved, "in."

"Why Yadin?" I asked.

He was excavating, fixing the pipes. Of course he was the hero of Masada—tall, thin—in looks, very similar to me.

"The man who digs?" I asked, more rhetorically than otherwise.

"Yes, that's right. He wants to break down the walls and make everything better and nice. Mm, that's interesting. Yes, that's it. When you help me with the dream everything comes out all right. Then," she laughed, "he dies, disappears. Boy, it's interesting! Marry you, let you do the work, break down the walls, a great idea! But the intercourse in the bathroom was strange. Reminds me of how good it feels to have a good bowel movement—get rid of the gas and then I don't smell. I remember reading Theodor Reik, and he tells of intercourse with a prostitute in a bathroom—very exciting, particularly as the girl's mother was in the next room. And now, what about those cigarette boxes, laughing, happy? I wanted to join in but didn't. Those cigarette people were so real I could even smell them and the flame of the matches."

(The reference to analysis was so pertinent, the television scene such a perfect rendering of her wish to enter the "glamorous" world of analysis, that I interrupted.)

"I smoke cigarettes here. The cardboard cigarettes weren't real, any more real than the analysis seems to you."

Everything seemed to float in air here. It bothered her that she was so uninvolved, just as with her boy friend. With him, she gave herself the excuse that she couldn't do two things at once, and because she was working on Sholem Aleichim, she couldn't find time for him.

Dinah's voice suddenly took on an altered quality, as though having given expression to her fantasies about me, something else could emerge. She talked of money, how much it was on her mind, her chances of getting a raise. "From cardboard boxes to paper money—but that's what I'm thinking about, really."

"Yes, that is quite real," I said.

She continued to talk of money, estimated costs, told how she planned to manage. She couldn't believe she had ever said that money wasn't important. Funny, it had been on her mind an awful lot. She'd even had a fantasy of "getting money in the age-old way of women."

Whereas I "used" the dream to help the patient distinguish between fantasy and reality, to foster the therapeutic alliance, the dream contained fantasies which hinted at pathology that interfered with her making a satisfactory heterosexual adjustment. Unquestionably, these fantasies emerged as a result of the change from psychotherapy to analysis, with the shift in character and depth of the transference. The combination of regression consequent to lying down and my subsidence into "passive" listening elicited fantasies of the primal scene, the fecal baby, and, finally, of prostitution.

10
Homosexual Libido
and the Dream

The psychological conditions under which little girls first experience love for their mothers, little boys for their fathers (or sisters and brothers) are as difficult to revive as other early events. Here again the dream, by widening the avenues of perception and attention, helps lift amnesia. The dream reflects the role of homosexuality in pathology and portrays with special clarity the ways in which it complicates the transference. The dream makes available for survey the homosexual conflicts of adolescence, a period too frequently relegated to analytic limbo. Through the dream and its interpretation, patients acquire a fuller recognition of the validity and significance of these crucial experiences.

Homosexual panic is among the most deleterious forms of anxiety we encounter in analysis and leads to formidable resistance. Broader intellectual and social acceptance of overt homosexuality increases rather than decreases the possibility of mismanaging the problem of its unconscious dynamic influence. The high-level concept of homosexuality not only has no value for the patient, but actually encourages resistance through intellectualization. Homosexuality becomes meaningful to a patient only when it is interpreted in terms of his own living experience.

Another warning against taking the manifest dream too literally may be in order here. A manifest dream element openly depicting homosexual activity may conceal the opposite or, by imagery and allusion, may express a latent thought far removed from sexuality.

The failure of one love affair after another, including two disastrous marriages, had originally propelled Jenny K. into analysis. She had wondered vaguely whether something was wrong with her as a female, but it was only after more than a year in treatment that intimations of an erotic interest in women began to make an appearance. Jenny found the idea of a homosexual affair inconceivable, although her appreciation of beautiful women was not totally devoid of sexual content and she could easily imagine how a man would consider such women desirable. Simultaneously, she discovered her interest in men to be more complicated than she had suspected. She presented this dream a few weeks after we had explored her masculine aspirations.[1]

A woman, a combination of cannibal and madam, has captured me and other girls and brought us to a farm or camp. She plans to eat us, but at the same time it is a sexual act. She will use us as prostitutes and slaves. The whole thing is sexually exciting, and even in the dream this is embarrassing.

[1] See dream, "Wants man's naval uniform" (p. 180).

The dream reminded her of games she used to play with other little girls enacting sexually exciting sadistic and masochistic scenes. In the dream, being in the woman's power had been stimulating. She remembered other details:

The woman was sitting in a chair, and a girl told me to go to her. I went running and leaping across a field. I was supposed to dance. The woman called, *"Élever,"* a dancing term, but I could not perform successfully. Then the scene changed to a harem. The madam is in a pool, says she is sexy and hungry, and leers obscenely at the lifeguard.

She thought it odd—first sex with a woman, then with a man. Sex and being hungry—that was herself, frustrated after abstinence. Being used for pleasure and unable to resist made her think of a man who almost raped her when she was in her teens. She had invited the overture and been thrilled by the experience. Leaping across the field reminded her that she had just been reading a book about a homosexual dancer. (A long pause broke the hitherto steady flow of associations.) Maybe she identified with him. Only yesterday her son asked her what a faggot was, and she had gone into an extended sociological-psychological explanation, only to discover he was referring to a stick of wood. The misunderstanding made her feel like an idiot. The girl in the dream who told her to go to the madam was actually a Lesbian dancer she knew.

In the silence that followed, I sensed an appreciable alteration in her mood. Tension suddenly filled the room, tension I knew to be born of anxiety.

"The idea that you might have homosexual inclinations frightens you," I said. "It might interfere with your feeling for men."

191

A veritable flood of associations poured forth. She talked of her difficulty with men, her need, even as a child, to be accepted not only as a girl but as one of the boys, her need to compete, to put men down, her lack of femininity. And now the promiscuity which she couldn't resist but which made her feel terribly ashamed.

My interpretation took into account the anxiety evoked by her associations. I wanted to help her overcome the resistance that recognition of homosexual impulses always produces. I intervened only when minimal assistance was required to bring the latent content of the dream from preconscious to conscious expression.

Two years of analysis brought George G. a little further along in his psychosexual development. As his involvement with me grew, various aspects of his latent homosexuality emerged. In addition to his identification with his mother came indications of a yearning for his father's love. The antecedent symbiotic identification with his mother yielded to his modeling himself in her likeness so that he could serve in her place as his father's lover. In part, these fantasies had been played out in childhood when he dressed in his mother's clothes and, like a woman, wiped himself from front to back after defecation. As he began to act out his latent homosexuality in derivative form under the influence of the transference, he had this dream:

> It was in a resort. I was looking for my room. There were men all around, no women. The men were very friendly. In each room there were two or three men. I had a towel wrapped around me but nothing else. It left my buttocks exposed.

He hadn't wanted to think of the dream after he woke up. He'd been in such a great mood yesterday. At the monthly board meeting, the director, a really great guy, took him aside to exchange a few pleasantries. Throughout the director's address, George, intoxicated by the intimacy he imagined existed between them, followed his remarks eagerly and winked at him several times in agreement.... He noticed that when disagreement arose between his wife and his friends he tended to be embarrassed by his wife and apologetic to the men.

"It's easier for you to agree with a man than with a woman," I said.

"In the dream I covered my buttocks. I don't like to think of the implications of that."

I called his attention to his slip—"covered" instead of "exposed," and added, "You have to cover up your feelings for a man."

He had certainly been thrilled when the director singled him out, thought how much better he would have liked it if only the two of them had been at the meeting. He remembered flicking towels at men's bare buttocks in the shower at college. He'd always felt drawn to men. Sometimes he felt they rebuffed him, as if he were being too eager. He knew his frequent questioning of me had a seductive quality. He wanted to know all about me. He had recently begun to feel more comfortable in his sessions.

I was glad I had eschewed the word "homosexual." No matter how sophisticated the patient, use of the word "homosexual" is dangerous. Hitherto, George's participation in analysis had been largely impersonal and academic. The progression of his associations suggested that, charged with the libidinal current of his homosexuality, positive transference was finally evolving. I certainly did not want to discourage this trend. The dream, and especially the slip, gave warning that beneath the positive current lingered the potential for future resistance. My reference to "covering up your feelings" anticipated and constituted a preparation for this eventuality.

Over the next months, George showed signs of rising sexual tension in the transference. On the one hand he repeatedly mentioned how comfortable he felt with me, on the other hand he worried lest he have an erection or emission while on the couch. I recognized in this a revival of his response to a seductive father. At the same time he reported numerous dreams with homosexual transference elements, but his associations did not permit me to interpret them on that basis. One of these has already been described.[2] Here is another:

> On a golf course, playing with another man behind me.
> I was zipping up my golf bag. He said, "Hurry, others are coming through." We teed off together and the balls went wild.

He spoke of golf, the other man's resemblance to himself, his lack of interest in his wife, of zipping up his fly in my bathroom. He also alluded tangentially to masturbation and, with more thought than feeling, to my penis and getting me to play with him.

The dream's homosexual connotations were clear enough, but the intellectual nature of his associations precluded intervention. I had to wait until something inescapably relevant would make an interpretation really

[2] See dream, "Intercourse on hospital operating table" (p. 178).

meaningful. Two days later, such an occasion presented itself. One of the relevancies was my interpretation of the following dream which he had the night after the hour just described.

A doctor invited me for a drink at a bar. I was very pleased but felt guilty that my wife wasn't there. Then I thought, "What the hell, I don't want to go back to her."

This time his associations[3] allowed me to interpret the dream directly: "You are much more interested in men than in women." He remained studiously aloof from the subject for the rest of the session and started the following day with:

I was in an old barber shop where I used to go with my father. My wife was with me. An old man with grey-white hair was going to give me a trim. I went to another man. But I wanted to get out of there with my wife.

After he left me yesterday he wanted to go home and have intercourse. That was pretty strange because his wife was menstruating, which always put him off. What he really wanted to do was show me he *was* interested in women.... All day he thought of what I'd said about his being more interested in men than in women.... A barber shop is where guys go. That old barber in the dream was me. When he used to go to the barber with his father, he wished he had a beard so he could be shaved like a man. Every time his wife took their son with her to the beauty parlor he got mad, thinking the kid would turn out queer.... The old barber shop used to have girlie magazines. He looked forward to the vacation when I wouldn't

---

[3] Unfortunately, I kept no record of these associations.

195

be around and he would be able to buy *Playboy Magazine* and jerk off.... He was going to introduce a girl who was looking for a job to a friend of his who needed a secretary. He hoped his friend would approve of her.

"The way to avoid the danger of homosexuality is to get busy with a woman," I said.

Instead of glib, "advanced" references to playing with me, or similarly contrived scenarios, George addressed himself to homelier subjects:

"I thought of that too. Getting involved with a girl so I won't be involved with a man. But it's superficial with any girl. Always more sincere with a man. My wife irritates me because she can't do things a man can do. How many times I've said I could be a better mother, a better housekeeper than she is."

Transference, the therapeutic alliance, and his associations encouraged me to speak directly about his homosexuality and to point out the defensive measures taken to meet the danger. Whereas the earlier dreams and associations had been pointing in the same direction, I waited for a propitious moment. I was, as always, guided by his ego state, and rather than precipitate resistance, preferred to give him time to absorb, in easy stages, the emerging homosexual content.

After his first marriage foundered, John Y. sought analytic help. While in treatment, and without the analyst's knowledge, he married again. The second marriage fell apart within months. The emotional conflict produced by the second marriage brought him to treatment with me. His subsequent relations with women had been superficial and equally brief. John defended himself against homosexual

wishes in the transference with either a hyperdiscreet aloofness or naked hostility. Outside analysis, he alternated
between heterosexual promiscuity and spurts of chummi-
ness with a younger man by whom he allowed himself to be
dominated. Acting out the libidinal oscillation kept the
homosexual current within bounds but left him in a state of
constant dissatisfaction. He presented this dream after a
frustrating weekend spent alone in his bachelor apartment.

> I was waiting to go into the men's room in a hotel or rail-
> road station. There was a crowd waiting to go in, all of
> them dressed in black. Nobody seemed able to enter.
> Then a watchman carrying a time clock came out and
> said, "Nobody is there." It seemed they had to empty
> it out because there was danger that a maniac had placed
> a bomb in it. Now we could go in.

He had talked to a girl in the lobby of a "hotel" adjoining
a "railroad station," but after some verbal interplay, decided not to get involved with her.... With an empty
weekend yawning before him, he thought of masturbating,
and after much debate decided it really wouldn't matter if
he did. He had been depressed ever since.

John gave no further direct associations to the dream. I
neither interpreted it nor intervened throughout the hour.
Resistance discouraged me from drawing his attention to
the dream's allusions to his conflict over masturbation and
homosexuality. In spite of his efforts to minimize masturbation ("nobody's there, it wouldn't matter if he did"), it
left him depressed (people "dressed in black"). He wanted
me ("watchman"-superego) to protect him against the
"dangerous bomb" in the "men's room." Both the "crowd"
and "nobody able to enter" bespoke no intervention for the
present. For all the information John's dream conveyed,

resistance made it impossible for me to share it with him. Despite a dream's richness and interest, despite its importance in connection with the problem we observe in the patient, only too often we have to keep its deeper implications to ourselves for future reference.

John's social life depended largely on his young friend Pete who rounded up the girls, organized the parties, and whose life seemed to be full of the purpose his own so conspicuously lacked. When John observed Pete more critically, he decided that the girls he provided were all mixed up and the parties never fulfilled their promise. In this context, he had the following dream:

> Pete and I were playing a game in a bar. He poured a glass of milky liquid on my back, then I poured one on his. I started to get mad and it didn't seem like a game any more. Then we were in an elevator which started going up faster and faster. Finally it shot through the roof into a skeletal framework which was open.

He and Pete had been so close lately that people were openly saying their relationship looked suspicious. He was beginning to see how hard it would be to break with him. . . . The milky liquid in the dream sounded like semen, and the elevator ride had undertones of sexual excitement attached to it. . . . He had felt awfully tense coming to his hour—angrier with me than usual.

I correlated this statement with the dream's reference to his getting mad, substituted myself for Pete, and said, "To fight with me is less disturbing than getting too close to me."

He recalled previous dreams of being attacked by men. He was beginning to feel more and more that his homo-

sexuality interfered—(he groped unsuccessfully for a minute or so but I said nothing). He felt less inclination to carry
on his meaningless charades with girls; they intuitively
suspected his gallantry, correctly interpreting it as spurious
and hostile.

John's omission of any reference to me indicated the
pressure of his resistance. Had I spoken about homosexuality, I would have played directly into the hands of his
major defense, intellectualization. He could talk easily
enough about the homosexual aspects of his friendship with
Pete. What he could not face was the transference expression of his homosexuality. If my intervention did not
succeed in bringing into the analytic situation what was
being acted out with Pete, it nevertheless brought him
closer to the heart of his problem.

Over the next weeks, John established a liaison with a girl
who had formerly been Pete's. He saw less of his friend
during this period, but as his ardor for the girl cooled he
turned back to Pete, who joined him in disparaging her. His
sessions, meanwhile, consisted chiefly of ruminations and
complaints concerning the sterility of his existence and the
failure of analysis to change anything. Then he had this
dream:

I was walking with someone toward a railroad car on a
siding in a railroad yard. We walked up steps leading into
the side. It was empty. The other person, a man, would
stay there while I went back for my sleeping bags. The
car wasn't going anywhere, and I didn't know if it ever
would. I looked for the sleeping bags in the station, then
down the road. They seemed to recede ever further away
in some other place and I had to return without them.

He described his growing misgivings about the girl. Yesterday he had even gone so far as to forget her name.

"Sleeping bags," I said.

He ignored this. He felt as if he were indeed going nowhere. He and Pete were back at their old stand, ticking off the women they knew and finding them wanting.

Had I referred to his abandonment of the woman in favor of the man, he would not have listened. Resistance demanded that my intervention be short and suggestive rather than explicit. I merely affirmed the emptiness of his affair. I would have to wait until, in the course of time, broader and deeper associations might lead him to the unconscious oedipal fantasies underlying his homosexual needs.

A certain brusqueness in speech, awkardness of gait, impatience with details, and propensity for taking charge gave evidence of Dinah B.'s rejection of her femininity. While still in psychotherapy, she told me of a brief homosexual affair she had in adolescence. This was followed by weeks devoted to working with her repressed homosexuality. During this time she began one day by announcing she had a great deal of ground to cover and an awful lot to say. Yesterday she finally started to menstruate, and last night she had a dream.

> A man is in prison together with a lot of other people, mostly men. They are all let out except for him. He has to stay on and on, occasionally let out, but having to return again for the rest of his life. I can see the years roll by as if numbered, 30, 40, 50, 60.

She woke up convinced the man was herself. I asked how she arrived at this conclusion. She couldn't say, but it was a very strong feeling, absolutely so. She had spent the day with a young man for whom she felt nothing and with whom she expected nothing to happen.

A pointedly evasive digression with no further mention of either menstruation or the dream led me to ask if she would tell me the dream again. She protested it would be repetitious; she had already given it in its entirety. After I asked how she could be so sure, she complied.

A man is in prison with a lot of other men. They are all left out except for him. He has to stay on and on for the rest of his life, left out only once in a while. The years roll by as if numbered, 30, 40, 50, 60. The man was medium height, short and unkempt with brown hair.

She remarked on the similarity between the man's physical characteristics and her own. I directed her attention to the emendation: "left out" instead of "let out." Now she remembered that yesterday she had been bothered by the persistent thought that all her friends were getting married and she was being "left" behind. She had been dismayed yesterday, when she rejected the young man by involuntarily withdrawing her hand from his. She had thought, "I'm always so much happier with girls than with boys."

"Being a woman," I said, "feels like a form of bondage for life, a bondage you can't escape. And one of the details of being a woman is menstruation which goes on and on. You know how little you care for details."

"It's true I never could stand scut work. I prefer to draw

up plans and leave the details to others." She devoted the rest of the hour to her fears of being attracted to women and finished reflectively with, "And I thought I couldn't get much from that dream except for the strong feeling I was the man. I certainly do leave out the details, don't I?"

We know that dream elements inserted as afterthoughts have special significance. By the same token, an altered version of a dream, second time around, calls particular attention to additions, subtractions, or alterations. Dinah's first version was a compromise between the idea seeking expression and her disinclination to express it—"Let's leave out that I feel left out." Her opening statement that she had so much to say (a protestation I privately reversed) influenced my decision for intervention. The need to deny her anatomical deficiency was the model for the typical defense of omitting details in favor of generalities. More often than not, the woman's "missing detail" can be traced to unconscious preoccupation with the missing penis. The man who possesses the detail can't be bothered with details. Fortunately for domestic harmony, the woman lacking it cares very much indeed.

For several months, Dinah said nothing at all about menstruation. Then, as if the hour just described had never occurred, she brought this dream:

> I am riding in a car with another woman. It gets dark and we stop at the corner of a deserted street. Suddenly a colored woman in a red coat gets in and starts to attack us. I don't know why.

She had spent the previous day with Gussie, her best friend, and stayed overnight with her. There had been a brief quarrel at bedtime when Gussie accused her of getting into bed like a Mack truck.

"When did you menstruate?" I asked.

How strange I should ask that. She usually forgot all about her periods. Only the fact that Gussie was menstruating reminded her that her own period was overdue. Then last night she found spots on her underwear. Curiously enough she had been sexually stimulated when she learned that Gussie was menstruating. She began to think of homosexuality and found herself flinching and withdrawing from contact with her. . . . If only menstruation could be ignored altogether.

Interpretation of the earlier dream was one of this dream's determinants and facilitated its interpretation, as did the homosexual connotations of "riding in a car with another woman" and the "red coat" which symbolized the phallic woman who must nevertheless menstruate. I read "I don't know why" as requiring the addendum, "this has to happen to me." I therefore chose to bring up, in question-form, the menstrual element symbolized in the dream to provide her with an opportunity for working with this critical facet of her latent homosexuality. The dream was instrumental in retrieving what might otherwise have remained inaccessible.

Early in analysis, several years before bringing the dream about to be cited, Don J., anxious to be exonerated from guilt, told me of having drawn his younger brother into sexual play when they were children. He alluded to the incident several times at widely scattered intervals and with obvious reluctance. Once he told me that his brother, an epicene man and possibly an overt homosexual, held him responsible for his abnormality.

Don himself had always been compulsively promiscuous with women, although he was repelled by their odors and secretions. The discovery, through analysis, of the reactive nature of his inordinate emphasis on cleanliness had been a revelation to him and was followed by the return from repression of anal fantasies acted out in intercourse, which no longer satisfied him unless accompanied by anal play. Up to the time of the first of these dreams, he had confined his activity to mutual insertion of fingers into the anus, although his fantasies ranged further. The connection between castration anxiety, homosexuality, and anal preoccupations had not yet been explored when Don reported this dream.

> I was working at a peculiar desk which was also an organ. It had a strange mechanism. In order for me to make music on it a man had to blow gas in at the back. This made the keys stand up. Otherwise, without the gas, the key just folded up and collapsed. A man was repairing the desk-organ.

Pseudo sophisticated comments on his "asshole" orientation were followed by complaints about the "shitty" smell in his apartment. He washed his hands constantly and changed the bed linen, but still the place seemed to stink. Last night he was so full of gas he had to leave the room throughout the evening to avoid farting in front of his girl. Last night too, something happened which really alarmed him. His girl agreed to let him insert his penis in her anus— the idea was tremendously exciting—but when it came to doing it, his erection subsided.

Don did not mention the "man" at the "back" or the "keys" which stood up and collapsed. (Absence of associations to symbolic elements in a dream is commonplace.) Long experience with him emboldened me to bypass the resistance inherent in extensive symbolization and to say, "A finger in your anus is all right and even exciting. Change finger to penis, in back of you."

He reflected a bit, then said, "Yeah, a man had to be around to fix the organ.... That repair man behind the organ was you. All weekend you were there. Is coming here the only way I can keep my prick up? With every woman I get sexless after a while."

The reference to me in his response was not very convincing, and I therefore did not follow it up. His easy acceptance of my rather blunt interpretation told me it had evoked anxiety and resistance. I said nothing further.

Six months later, Don had a dream which made him feel physically ill. When he woke up he had to clean the whole apartment to get rid of anything dirty. His old stiffness was so bad he had to do exercises to loosen up. On his way to my office, he had walked so stiffly he was reminded of his brother whose affected gait proclaimed for miles around what he was.

I made a tape of family voices. I prized it highly as a memento. I was furious with some boys who got hold of it behind my back. They erased the sound track.

Then I was drinking warm beer in a bathroom with several men. It was revolting and I wanted to vomit. Then I was recalling a dream in great detail, even while I was dreaming. I knew I was dreaming of a dream, and yet it was as real as if it were actually happening. I was having sexual relations with my brother. It was a definite sweet love affair as between two adults and not between kids.

Note the progression of the dream: from expunging the memory to a desire to expel it completely, ending with a restatement of the actual childhood episode contained in the dream within a dream—attempts at defense, yielding to expression of the wish.

Don emphasized that the last scene had affected him most profoundly. It was as if a hidden love affair had been going on for months and years, as if he had known about it all along but had never acknowledged it. . . . He wished he could bring himself to think of marrying. That other people could marry and be happy but not himself made him feel deformed. He had dinner with his girl friend and his brother last night and, as usual, squirmed with uneasiness, unable to decide to which of them his loyalty belonged. For a long time he had been noticing how inhibited he was when alone with his brother—stiff and self-conscious; he wanted a girl to be with them. The same thing happened when he was with other men. . . . That dream within the dream about his love affair with his brother had been so real. It seemed so even after he woke up; he had remained motionless, rigid, felt paralyzed.

"Keeping yourself on guard against these unwelcome homosexual feelings can take a physical form. It makes you stiff."

He groaned, "I can't sit comfortably in the same room with him. I get so rigid with fear I want to shriek. Yesterday I asked my girl if she thought the lively colored shirts and suits I like were too swishy. She reassured me it was the going thing and perfectly all right. Why can't I marry? Why do I treat sex as if it were dirty?"

I thought a correlation of his anxiety with the physical symptoms that caused him so much anguish would help Don over a hurdle without adding to the anxiety which so obviously held him in its grip. He was working through adequately, and further pursuit of other elements in the dream would have been gratuitous.

11
The Oedipal Conflict and the Dream

Some patients present themselves to us as having sprung full-blown onto a scene burdened with husbands, wives, children, friends, enemies and of course, symptoms; for all we are told, they never had parents, siblings, or a childhood. With such patients the dream, which regularly revives infantile sexual or aggressive events having to do with parents or their surrogates, may constitute our sole means of reconstructing the past. Most oedipal fantasies have always been unconscious. Even those that attain preconscious recognition and verbal expression (I love you, Mommy; I hate you, Daddy) later succumb to repression. By reanimating repressed memories, the dream encourages the patient to focus his attention on the neglected period.

As the transference evolves, we learn of the past through the present. Nowhere is this more evident than with dreams which refer to the oedipal situation. We therefore expect that our interpretation of dreams with oedipal content sometimes will be made in terms of the transference, sometimes will stress the original content directly. The dream helps sort out which aspect is more pertinent and active when, as so often happens in analysis, past and present are indistinguishable.

In waking life, repression of oedipal conflicts results in separation of hostile impulses toward the person of the same sex from erotic urges toward one of the opposite sex. Similarly in dreams, censorship and the dream work disguise the connection between the two sides of the oedipal drama, or perhaps positive and negative aspects will appear in stages, either in dreams of the same night or successive nights. Nevertheless, connections are easier to make by means of the dream, in spite of censorship and distortion, than they are when the two aspects are presented seriatim in acting out or are kept apart by isolation of their affects. The inappropriateness of the infantile impulses is seen more clearly from a dream than from acting out. By lending distance, the dream makes it easier for the patient to view his impulses as ego-alien.

Inasmuch as the oedipal period of development lays the ground for the definitive flowering of the superego, we are not surprised to find that whenever and wherever oedipal impulses are aroused, a superego response is activated. In the dreams that follow, we shall be concerned as much with response as with impulse, our emphasis in interpretation depending on which is foremost and active at the time.

Acting out of unconscious conflicts often presents intransigent problems until it is made ego-alien. All unconscious conflicts are subject to acting out, but none more fatefully or repetitiously than the oedipal, so unrewarding in its avid pursuit of what passes for happiness. When transference reactivates oedipal cravings, acting them out elsewhere can succeed in keeping their true significance at bay. Dreams help restore the oedipal resurgence to its proper place in the analytic process, the transference, where the provenance of oedipal impulses can be more appropriately reconstructed and evaluated. By resurrecting the actual objects and events of the oedipal period together with their related affects, the dream is an indispensable ally in bringing the patient closer to his unconscious. In the dream, as in transference, the drama of oedipal development becomes a living reality, not merely an intellectual exercise.

While we were still working face to face, Dinah B. greeted me one day with an oddly guarded air.

"Any trouble?" I asked.

Nothing particular; she was just upset about her job. Her boss was due back from vacation, and he was so demanding he would probably complain she hadn't done her work properly during his absence and make her feel terribly guilty. Then too, she was irritable and tense from having spent the weekend with her parents. They had just returned from vacation, her mother looking positively dilapidated and acting the martyr. She would have preferred a weekend in her own apartment, but her mother so obviously expected her to be with them, what could she do?

"Isn't it strange how accountable you feel to your mother," I said.

"What is this guilt I always feel?" she answered quizzically. "But I don't want to go on with this. I have a dream I want to tell you."

211

I am in a room which seems to have a fire in it. I can't see it, but the room is getting warm. People are packing up and leaving. I'm the last one to get out. I'm wearing an elegant evening dress with earrings, all made up.

I used as associations the information which preceded the dream (with an involuntary flashback to Dora's dream of escape from the burning room with her jewels [Freud, 1905]) and said, "You were getting heated up in the dream. You were elegant and your mother was so dowdy. What better way to express an argument with her."

Dinah paused reflectively, then continued. Last night after dinner, her mother started to give herself a manicure. Her father asked if she would do his nails, too. Dinah felt strangely embarrassed as she watched the two of them. Later, back in her own apartment, she thought of masturbating. The notion that her parents were probably being sexually active flashed across her mind.... How could they—how could *he*—with such an unattractive woman?

The fire in the dream condensed Dinah's aggression with her wish to masturbate and the oedipal implications of both. Guilt she "didn't want to talk about" hung in the air and stemmed as much from her impulse to masturbate as from oedipal rage at her mother. But this I discovered only after I made my interpretation.

Two months later Dinah again looked so preoccupied and ill at ease that I asked her what was wrong. She didn't know, but she wondered why, after all this time in treatment, she continued to feel so awkward in my waiting-room. She had a dream to tell me.

I was pregnant. I felt very ashamed because I wasn't married. It seemed I had had one night of love several months ago. I didn't know who the father was. I wondered how I could get rid of it. I remembered the intercourse felt very good and kept thinking about it. It bothered me most of all that it would show and people would know.

She recalled having dreamed of being pregnant once before. . . . The father wasn't anyone in particular. She was lonely, frustrated, and wanted to make love with someone. . . . It seemed like a long time since her last hour with me . . . the weekend had seemed longer than usual. She remembered talking about sexual inhibitions last time she was here. She had been thinking of me and felt very stupid to have to say that she observed what I wore and had fantasies of buying clothes for me.

"You were embarrassed at being pregnant and you were embarrassed coming here to see me," I said.

"You mean there's some connection? Well, I did think of masturbating this weekend, but I didn't do it." Now she recalled additional details in the dream:

I went to a man for help to get an abortion. He would give me money. My mother was in the dream somewhere.

When she was about six years old, her mother had found her playing doctor with a little boy and had scolded her severely. . . . Going to a man for help made her think of coming to me for help. The man in the dream had been the father of the child.

"In your loneliness and frustration you could think of being pregnant, having a child as consolation. I would be the one to whom you would apply for such help—to give you this baby."

213

Her response consumed the remainder of the hour: She was so lonely, almost any man would do. And yet, to have intercourse with just anybody was inconceivable. To have intercourse before marriage was equally unthinkable, and yet she had been thinking of it. It was hard to imagine her dream had to do with wanting a baby from me. She had heard of these things—little girls wanting babies from their fathers. Maybe that's why she remembered her mother's scolding so vividly.

I hoped, by making connections and comparing her different statements, to gradually lead her to the inevitable conclusion she herself had to draw from the dream.

John Y. defended himself against depression by engaging in a frenzy of sexual activity unconsciously calculated to depress him still further. His search for girls was endless. Not satisfied with those he met at work, he sought girls by joining social organizations and picked up others at bars. John's other major activity consisted of finding ways to provoke the people he worked with, especially his superiors. This had already cost him several good jobs. Guilt and self-recrimination subsequent to this oedipally derived treadmill immobilized him until loneliness forced him to repeat the cycle. Analysis had so far succeeded in modifying recurrent spasms of acting out. He now curbed himself sufficiently at work to retain his job and no longer married the girls. The following dream occurred after I had tried, not for the first time, to make him see the connection between his inappropriate and self-destructive performance and his defiance of his superego.

> I was having intercourse with my daughter. She seemed somewhat surprised but compliant. I hesitated but went ahead anyway.

He woke up wondering where such an extraordinary dream came from. The previous evening he was with friends much younger than himself who, like adolescents, had thrown aside their inhibitions to enjoy a modified orgy. He both envied and suspected their lack of restraint, so in contrast with his own need, just then, to remain the passive observer. Watching them, he was seized with a sudden revelation: his *ersatz* inhibitions were unnecessary; it was time he threw off this burden. Yet he couldn't help feeling guilty. In the dream he had held back, unable to go through it without qualms. If only he could get rid of his constraint, shed the feeling of guilt which prevented him from acting naturally.

"You try to convince yourself that you have nothing to be afraid of, that nothing can shock you. And your dream has you doing something forbidden, something you know you shouldn't do."

"Yeah. It reminds me of when I was a kid. My father traveled a lot, and whenever he left, my first thought was 'Who will punish me now?' and I would let myself go, masturbating and having all sorts of erotic daydreams."

Throughout more than three years of analysis, John had rarely mentioned his family or childhood, confining himself instead to talk of his job, his dates, and what he had done over the weekend.

The manifest content of the dream might have suggested that the dream work had gone on vacation, the depths of the unconscious had finally been plumbed, and a repressed impulse had broken through all defenses. Far from reflecting a wish for intercourse with his daughter, however, John's dream incorporated a superego component which reminded him of its continued presence and power by confronting him with the image of a forbidden incestuous scene. It was in effect a distorted version of his attempts both to defy his superego ("look what I can do—I'm not guilty") and to invoke its support against the uncontrolled infantile drive for incestuous gratification.

As a concomitant to his brief but numerous sexual forays, John maintained sporadic communication with one of his past mistresses, a doctor's wife some years older than himself. In the course of describing a recent visit to her, he referred glancingly, almost furtively, to sexual fantasies involving my wife.

"You feel guilty," I said, "because you are taking the woman who belongs to me."

He accepted my remark with obvious reluctance and that night dreamed:

> I was lying in bed when suddenly my father came in. He stood quietly, but I began to scream and rage. I didn't know what I was saying. There was no reason, no idea, no content to it. I just raged at him.

He was appalled at the venom of his attack, particularly as he was convinced that I was its real object.

"First you dismiss me and take my wife. Then you are furious with me. Your interest in the woman is a fight with the man," I said.

"Hmm, maybe. Yesterday after I left you, I flew into a completely uncalled-for rage at my boss. I was so mad I didn't care about the consequences. Later, I was aghast at what I'd done and couldn't imagine what prompted me. It was as if I had been asking to be fired. And then I had that dream. Hmmm."

On a superficial level, his rage at me (the dream work, having disguised the object and stripped the affect of content, permitted the rage to come through) was stimulated by the intervention of the previous hour, but I chose an interpretation which incorporated both transference and its suggestive oedipal undertones because of his fantasies and his reluctance to accept my intervention of the day before.

A year later, John was acting out a new version of the oedipal situation, this time with a girl almost young enough to be his daughter. Like the doctor's wife, this girl was committed to another man. After we had spent some weeks in analysis of this phase of resistance in his acting out, he reported this dream:

> I am in a meeting with other people. Something important is about to happen. I feel my boss is going to make some sort of aggressive move. As usual, I pretend I don't care and am superior to the rest of the people. Then he announces he is sick and is going to leave the firm of his own accord, without being pushed.

He thought his "retiring boss" was actually me: he so often thought of quitting not only his job but analysis. He wondered how his current affair would end; it was pleasant, but he felt "half-and-half" about wanting it to continue.... In the dream there had been a hint of his boss having a heart attack. Strange, the difference between what he expected the boss to say and what he did say. A funny thought intruded: he was grateful to me for my dependability, for not getting sick, not being capricious.... He found himself calling his girl by the wrong name—kept using the name of the doctor's wife.... Maybe with the reorganization at the office, he would be put in charge of the new department.

"I'm feeling almost euphoric today," he continued, "nothing bothers me. It's so nice with X. She is the ideal person to romance with—no wish to settle down. Hmmm, in that dream—time for you to retire."

"To be dead," I said.

"Well, that's not what the dream said, but nevertheless it was a pretty serious condition my boss had. Cancer. Three months to live." Then, grudgingly, "You're right."

"You can live happily ever after with your girl, with me out of the way."

"Right!" he said promptly. "It fits in a lot of ways. Getting rid of you is like getting rid of the old man.... What a funny process this is," he added reflectively.

John's driving passion, to do what he clearly knew ought not be done, derived from unconscious patricidal impulses. To kill his superego was to kill his father. The most telling connections, the most elegant constructions, the most elaborate interpretations could not convince him that his defensive maneuvers to escape guilt were futile. Not so with the dream.

A few days later John had this dream during a night spent with his girl:

I was in a restaurant. Nobody there but a waitress. I sat alone. The waitress beckoned and I followed her to a back room. She pointed to a refrigerator where I saw my daughter crouching, half frozen. I said, "What the hell is going on here?" I picked her up, breathed on her neck, and carried her out. She was scared, half frozen, but grateful to me.

He spoke at length about his girl. Full of solicitude, he had covered her as she slept so she wouldn't be cold, looked at her, thought how young she was, so like a child, like his own daughter. He told her his dream, and they both decided they couldn't see what it had to do with her. (That he had already discovered the unconscious connection between the girl and his daughter was clear. He not only denied it, but told the girl his dream.) He wondered what he was up to, fooling around with someone her age.

I proceeded on the principle that spoken words, a contribution from the superego, derive from something heard, spoken, read, or thought, and processed by the dream work.

" 'What the hell is going on here?' were spoken words?" I asked.

"Yes. And there was something about the words that seemed very real, very significant somehow."

"Where do they come from?"

"I can't put my finger on it. Yet I know something just like this has been going on in my mind. I've been asking myself what I'm doing . . ."

" . . . with the girl. A part of you calls yourself to account for what you are doing."

"What do I need a dream for, to tell me something I knew all along?"

Both this dream and the one in which he had intercourse with his daughter[1] contained superego recriminations for oedipal impulses and acting out—the earlier dream, with a counterphobic defense, "who's afraid?" The last dream, despite defense, indicated that anxiety was present ("she was scared" meant he was). My intervention aimed at emphasizing the contribution made by his unconscious sense of guilt to the unsatisfactory nature of his sexual relationship with the girl. Oedipal guilt remained the

---

[1] See dream, "Intercourse with his daughter" (p. 214).

deepest source of his pathology. The dream helped bring into analysis what John was acting out with so little satisfaction.

John reported the following dream after listening to his adolescent son describe a successful sexual exploit.

> I wandered through an old house like a barn. It was full of old, broken-down furniture. On the second floor, I saw a table. When I came close, I saw it was an old sewing table. I thought I might be able to use it. Then I saw the top was gone, but the legs were still holding on with screws. I thought it a shame. It was well made. I knew I couldn't put it together again. It had been done by a skilled man who should have handed down his skill to his son.

He reflected ruefully that he was not doing nearly so well as his son.... Why was it other people could marry, stay together, while all he ever seemed to do was spend his time with beat-up, run-down types? Other people had "well-made" marriages, they could talk to each other; he couldn't.... Had his father and mother?

"You must have always wanted to do what your father and mother did," I said, "but your father could and you couldn't."

"That again?" from him. Then he remembered a second dream:

> I was sitting at a table with my mother. She made some remark, pleasantly, about something I might do. I slammed a knife into the table and said, "I'll do what I want when it happens. That'll be a change. It will come." I wasn't sure what.

The rich symbolism in the first dream pointed clearly to its oedipal sources. His associations provided confirmation. The interpretation helped bring the second dream to the surface.

" 'Knife in the table' is sexual, isn't it? But that sounds so academic."

I could not have agreed more. Again, he called into play his specific method of defensive resistance: the substantive truth followed by complete dismissal. John's reconstitution of his son in his own father's image was far from academic.

No one could be blamed for thinking that a great deal of work with John went for very little in the way of reducing defenses and resistance, particularly isolation. To inch along with him might well raise the question of whether the dream has anything to offer after all. But without his dreams, I would have had almost no access to crucial events of his infancy, childhood, and relations with his family. His dreams were instrumental in stimulating associations that enabled me to undo his defensive isolation and retrieve the meaningful affect belonging to his oedipal conflict. I had more than enough evidence that his sexual promiscuity stemmed less from inordinate appetite than from his unconsciously acted-out need to defy me as reconstituted father-superego. Interpretations to this effect produced grudging intellectual acceptance. The dream testimony was another matter, an interior message he could not evade.

Considerable time spent in analytic pursuit of the sources of Paul D.'s sexual and marital dissatisfaction came to a head in connection with the following dream. He started the hour saying he had a vivid dream to tell me, one which had awakened him before dawn and disturbed him so much he could not get back to sleep. Because Paul generally treated his dreams as visitations from another planet, having nothing to do with him, his preface in itself was significant.

> I was in a place to which I was returning after many years. I knew I had been there before, recently, too. There was a girl, smiling, with a beautiful figure, to whom I was strongly attracted. I sat on a bed with my father and bitterly told him I wanted to marry her but couldn't. I was already married. My father looked sad as though he were grieving for me and wanted to help.

He had avoided his wife last night by going out with a friend after dinner. When he got home, his wife told him his father, concerned over his mother's health, had telephoned. Paul upbraided himself for his negligence and, at his wife's urging, returned his father's call. Their entire conversation revolved around his mother's illness.... He was still troubled by extramarital fantasies. The only way he could work up an appetite for his wife was by thinking of another woman.

(I thought a gap still existed between what he was saying and what the dream told me lay in his unconscious. In order to make the connection between the dream and associations more meaningful, I asked if he could help out any further with the dream. He obliged by concentrating on the girl.) She was unknown and yet familiar; he had the odd feeling he had known her before; his attraction to her had an inevitable, compelling quality.

Paul's associations drifted off to the various girls he had known before he was married. After he continued in this vein for some time, I concluded he had gone as far as he

could without help and was ready to assimilate an interpretation.

"Last night you talked to your father about your mother.
In your dream you talked to him about a woman you
wanted to marry."

His voice rose sharply, "Yes, it was mother, the girl I
can't marry. After all this, it comes down to my mother. I'm
the mama's boy all right. I always thought of my mother as
pretty, young. I particularly remember thinking what a
good figure she had. This is what you hear about of
course. . . . So this is what I'm so unhappy about—all those
other girls."

Recognition in the manifest dream of symbolic rendering
of the oedipal drama (the place one has been in before and
to which one returns—mother) does not give us license to
submit our findings to the patient without first taking the
necessary and sufficient intermediate steps. By confronting
Paul with a source of his sexual discontent, so poignantly
expressed in the dream, I neither anticipated nor observed a
dramatic change of any kind. Ongoing defenses resulted in
renewed repression, but the message had come through.

One of Don J.'s dominant complaints centered on his
inability to sustain a meaningful attachment to any woman. He could go through the motions of courtship easily
enough, but real zest came only when he knew the woman
belonged to another man. One day he threw himself down
on my couch with the announcement that he was about to
tell me a very vivid dream, the scene of which, he wanted
me to understand, was something that had permeated his
entire life and would not leave him.

> I am introduced to a new girl. She is sexually exciting. I kiss and embrace her and it's delightful. I avoid going all the way. Then I am at a restaurant next day and see her with another man. I am furious and heartbroken. I get up. I have to know the truth. I go out. But to make sure of what I see I take a last look. She *is* with the other man.

He woke up full of hate, felt like screaming, and wanted the scene to go away, but it wouldn't. No matter how much he went over the many ways we had looked at this thing before, it didn't help. He knew, of course, that he was attracted to women only if they belonged to someone else. His present girl was so devoted to him he was edgy with her and wanted out.... Yesterday he had a violent argument with a woman who hadn't paid him for work he had done for her. He couldn't get rid of the feeling that she preferred other men to him. Why was he always in competition with men? Obviously, it was related to the dream.

"Such a strong feeling," I said, "must come from more than one place. You know how far back it goes. Who is the girl who goes with another man?"

He knew the problem went back to his mother. It had to, but it didn't help to be academic. Besides, his mother actually gave him a pain. His father was much the nicer person. Why couldn't he get excited by a woman he felt tenderness for? Why did sex with a woman have to mean a fight with a man? Why did he always conjure up competition even when it didn't exist? Why did he always have to make a scene like in the dream? That woman who hadn't paid him—the woman who promises but doesn't give—was like his mother.

Don's as-if character and narcissism raised doubts concerning the reality-in-depth of any of his feelings. It also created obstacles for him in distinguishing between fantasy and reality in the analysis as elsewhere. A dream so explicit, so seemingly without distortion, might well arouse an analyst's suspicions. It could easily give the impression of having sprung from compliance rooted in resistance. The course of the hour nevertheless attested to the dream's validity, as did the dream he had that night:

> I am stuck with my girl near Boston and want to get away. To my delight and relief, I see my mother and father coming in a station wagon. I know I am saved.

He had wanted to call me, after he left yesterday, to tell me what a genius I was. It had stayed with him all day—that unavailable woman. He'd heard it all before, but yesterday it seemed to stick, and then last night this dream, this relief with his parents. He wanted to see them, he was happy with them, in the dream. He remembered when he was at summer camp; it was near Boston. He was so homesick he wouldn't let his mother leave. He complained and carried on so that she told him he was making her life miserable.

He paused. "This is what I do with all my women now. I make them miserable until they complain, asking me what I want."

Fairly early in her analysis, Jenny K. brought this dream:

> I was in this office. As I was going out the door, I saw I was naked. In the hall on the table were my brassiere and panties. But there were two brassieres, one belonging to the woman now waiting to see you. I thought, "She shouldn't do that too. I'm your patient." You came out to

explain things to her but you were someone else, a man I knew when I was a child. I said to you-him, "Tell about my father; you know the family."

She was embarrassed at her nakedness in the dream (as she spoke she crossed her arms over her bosom, then observing herself, laughed self-consciously and admitted to sexual fantasies about me which made her uneasy). She was equally mortified to think her dream had changed me into a man she had always thought of as a weakling. She always seemed to end up with effeminate men. Her father let himself be dominated by her mother.... She was very much like her mother.... A friend had just called to say she had looked me up and found me eminently qualified. The friend was in treatment with a psychologist, and Jenny wondered whether the call had been inspired by jealousy.... She longed to know all about me.... She was quite sure I was a real man.... Her feelings for her father vacillated so. One moment he was her hero, the next a fallible simpleton. She couldn't remember when it hadn't been like that. "I was a handful. Mother couldn't manage me. She would say to father, 'Tell her, tell her.' But he wouldn't put his foot down, not even when I paraded naked around the house."

Jenny's associations flowed freely enough to make intervention superfluous, and I observed one of the physician's guiding principles contained in the old medical maxim, *primum non nocere*—above all things, do no harm. I might have correlated the jealousy mentioned in her associations with her jealousy in the dream; I might have offered the interpretation, "You want me all to yourself"; I might have drawn the obvious parallel between her attitude to her father and to me; I might have called her attention to her curiosity about me, both professional and sexual. I chose to say nothing. The dream and associations were, first of all, an invitation to act out the oedipal drama with her. My silence served a double purpose: first, to refuse the invitation; second, to avoid premature interpretation based on associations as yet too diffuse. The associations, while perfectly valid, were in themselves a seductive appeal. Had I yielded with an intervention, I would have foreclosed the opportunity for further development of the oedipal conflict in the transference.

The emphasis Simon E. placed on money could not be accounted for solely on the basis of anality or identification with a father whose byword was, "What does it cost?" One source of his preoccupation became clearer when I learned that, as a child, he had consistently seduced his mother into giving him money which his father as consistently denied him.

The day before the first of these dreams, he asked if I would write to his insurance company to prod them into sending him money due him for my bill. I declined, told him his request could be compared with his attempts to get money from his parents, and specifically added that he was trying to assign their roles to me. This led him to talk about the competition between himself and his father. The next day he reported this dream:

> I was in a large room with several beds in it, like a hospital. A small boy was being nasty or naughty. He was being kept home and not allowed to go to the movies. He began to act up. I said to him, "Go to your room! Go to bed!" He went.

He had so much to say that was left over from his last hour.... He used to love hanging around his father when he was small, but no matter what he did, his father criticized him and made him feel inadequate. Now he was working his head off to make a lot of money and, though he was doing well enough, couldn't help feeling he didn't deserve it.

Simon's dream was plainly instigated by my refusal to accede to his request and the transference interpretation accompanying my refusal.

"You consider yourself incompetent, just as your father did. You agree with him. And you took as criticism what I said to you yesterday."

For the first time since starting analysis, he broke into uncontrollable sobs which continued for the rest of the hour, accompanied by an outburst of bitter resentment. He raged at his father for failing to understand him, for belittling him, for making him feel inadequate and guilty, when he knew he was as good as anybody and better. "I haven't cried like this for years. I'm not clear why I'm crying, but I can't stop."

That night he had another dream.

> I'm saying goodby to my parents who are sitting in a car. It's very painful. They drive off. Then I go to my wife but my father is with her. He looks very old, his teeth are rotting, like an old hill man. Then I'm in a hotel room and want to take a shower with my wife. I have a big erection—a gigantic one—and say to her, "Look how big my penis is now." I thrust it in her but lose the opening. I finally fuck her standing up. The strange thing is, someone else is standing around.

It was odd, in connection with yesterday's dream he had so many thoughts about his father but didn't mention his mother. Yesterday exhausted him so much he couldn't cry anymore. Though he knew he'd only scratched the surface, the pressure was off a little.... How often he accommodated himself to his father and at the same time tried to outdo him. "I was Miss Goody Two Shoes. I felt like a sissy. I couldn't be a regular guy."

"What about the large penis in the dream? You stressed that."

"It reminded me of a horse. With such a penis I could do anything. In the dream my wife took it in her hand and her breasts were larger than they really are."

Simon's previous description of his mother provided the basis for my next question: "Like your mother's?"

Only yesterday he had been thinking about her body. He'd seen her breasts when he was in his teens; she often talked about how big they were. There had been the familiar bathtub routine when she coddled his penis, calling it a cute little birdie. The third person in the bed (another revision) must have been his mother. He saw why he felt guilty with his father and brother. He had loved his mother dearly in those days and hadn't wanted anyone else around. He felt half asleep as he talked to me, as if he were still dreaming. "If I make enough money I won't need them. That would be my vengeance."

"In your dream you remarked how big your penis is now, implying a contrast with another time."

"I still feel it is small, like that cute little birdie."

"With your big mother you must have felt it to be very small, compared with your father's. And the vengeance you mention must be connected with making up for that."

A reflective silence appropriated the remaining minutes of the hour. Although I never made a specific connection between his fight with his father and his intractable obsession with money, shortly after this, the subject temporarily receded into the background.

Six months later, Simon started an hour with this dream:

> I was in a room with my father. He was sarcastic and belittled psychiatry. I tried to quiet him but he wouldn't listen. I had to fight with myself to control my fury. I wanted to tell him he wasn't fair.

He remembered my once having said he wasn't being fair to me. He also recalled his diatribes against me and his frequent complaints that I didn't know what I was doing. His father in the dream was both himself and me, that he knew. He had another dream:

> I was with a friend and asked him for the phone number of a woman we both knew. It was a curiously long number. He looked at me quizzically but gave me the number.

Yesterday he had found himself defending his father against someone who was disparaging him. Yet, afterwards, he couldn't help having all sorts of vengeful fantasies about the old man and me.... The telephone number reminded him of his mother's number out of town.

I supplied the link to what had been kept apart:

"You fight with your father, then get your mother. The two go together."

12
Adaptive Ego and Superego in the Dream

The preceding sections have included a number of dreams in sequence to show, among other things, how the dream reflects fluctuations in ego-defensive functioning. I have also referred, if sometimes only in passing, to the role played in the dream by both ego and superego in their opposition to instinct. I want now to examine in greater detail the contribution to the dream of the adaptive and creative aspects of the ego and superego.

Analysis cannot be successfully conducted without the help of a portion of the ego which stands apart from the turmoil of conflict and, in relative neutrality, casts a level look at all aspects of the situation. Eventually a conflict-free, autonomous ego comes to the patient's and our assistance by drawing a distinction between past and present, fantasy and reality, the reasonable and the un-reasonable, the self and others. It can, in short, see what is truly alien to its own best interests. And since we can do nothing without an ego which, to some extent, takes this position, psychoanalysis attempts first of all to foster and strengthen the ego's conflict-free, autonomous functions, to make pathology ego-alien. In treating character disorders, this, as well as the repair of superego defects, may indeed take up most of our time.

We do not expect shifts in the patient's dynamic equilibrium to be accompanied by dramatic changes in his symptoms or overt behavior. Growth and development of conflict-free functions of the ego, as well as modifications in the superego, are internal processes, moving imperceptibly over extended periods of time without announcing their arrival. The clinical silence in which the sometimes agonizingly slow rate of change occurs gives us ample time to doubt the effectiveness of our procedures.

Inasmuch as dreams, like symptoms, are compromises between the demands of the structural systems, the nature of the compromise will reflect the qualitative and quantitative alterations in the systems themselves. Dreams often herald a growing capacity for the recognition of reality, for containment of impulse, for the formation of fresh identifications. Their interpretation thereby gives us insights into impending change of function brought about by the modification in the nature and distribution of unconscious forces before we see changes in the clinical picture.

As the ego acquires new powers of synthesis, perception, integration, regulation, and control; as the superego functioning advances from a punitive to a more idealistic level, we can, without neglecting the dream from below, increasingly turn our attention to the dream from above. Without losing sight of the past, our interpretations can take into greater account the meaning and reality of the present.

As a result of analysis, Don J. began to regard his compulsive promiscuity as grotesque and his deception of the girl who loved him as indefensible. He could examine his fantasy-ridden impulses with a degree of objectivity that made everything he did seem unreal, but he nevertheless continued to act them out. Two days after I had said to him, "You don't treat what you do here as real,"[1] he brought a highly condensed and symbolically disguised dream.

> I had my camera and was trying to load it. I couldn't
> get the reel in. It was full of junk, bits of paper and food.
> I was sweating with it and woke up that way.

Last night he had done it again. He had a telephone conversation with a woman he really despised. The filth they exchanged! And it was as much his doing as hers. When he hung up he was absolutely disgusted with himself. ... All women were beginning to look alike to him—nothing seemed real.

"You couldn't get the real thing in," I said, "paper and food are the dream's way of referring to women. You try to get your penis to work by concentrating on filth, dirt, junk, but it doesn't work."

"Sure, I know that camera is my penis—we had it once before. Jesus, what am I doing anyway?"

Don was already aware of the anxiety produced by aggression, but only dimly conscious of the relation be-

[1] See p. 120.

tween anxiety and his sexual promiscuity. That he was now having trouble sustaining an erection unless certain conditions were fulfilled constituted, in a psychoanalytic sense, a definite advance in one who had heretofore made a virtue of sexual infallibility. A comparison of this session with one already described,[2] which occurred a half year before, might prove interesting.

Six months later, Don was still belaboring himself for his voracious lusts, his indifference to his devoted girl, and the recrudescence of uncontrollable outbursts of temper at his parents. For the first time in his life he was using four-letter words to them. Why was this happening to him, he asked. When was he going to get over it? Maybe he needed a new analyst? When was this one going to help?

He treated me to several days of stony silence, canceled an appointment ostensibly for business reasons, and then reported this dream:

> I was in a hotel room like the one my degenerate uncle lived in. I lay on a bed and was eating scrambled eggs. X walks in to leave something for me. I didn't get up to greet him or respond cordially—I was rude. He took a burn and started to leave. I got into a panic that I offended him. I followed him out into the hall. I didn't want our friendship to be ended. I apologized, pleaded, was servile, said I was sorry, that I wasn't well.

He liked X, a nice, friendly guy. He didn't know who he stood for, but was disturbed that relations with him would be cut off.

"Yesterday you and I were cut off," I said.

He had wanted to be here yesterday. What bothered him

---

[2] See dream, "Eats paper" (p. 154).

most in the dream was his fear that relations with the man would be broken off. That was the point of the dream. And he sat there eating, letting him wait; then he realized he had goofed; after all, the guy was human and couldn't be treated that way. . . . He remembered telling me the other day of sitting and arguing with his father. When he had said, "I felt like getting off the couch and hitting him," I had called attention to his saying "couch." He realized I meant his hostility toward me. He hadn't missed that! It bothered him that with all I had said and all he knew, nothing had changed. He'd had a second dream, too:

> Frank Sinatra—we're together, social, fishing. I'm thrilled to be with the Chairman of the Board—the most publicized figure in the world. I'm in with him (I really don't understand these dreams)—he's on my level.

Sinatra—he read that Sinatra had been hit in a brawl. A man with so many women, with everything, to be so violent, so full of tantrums, must be miserably unhappy. And that luncheon he had to attend yesterday—all those married men saying, "I'd like to lay that broad,"—so much sexual unrest—what was wrong with everybody? That fishing in the dream was no accident. Lately he'd taken to fishing with his father. But there was more glamour with Sinatra than with his father. In both dreams he was with a man. Being with a man cut him off from women. Last night he got angry at his girl, couldn't wait for her to leave. And she took such great care of him, even his mother told him the other day, "You're crazy if you don't marry her; she's unbelievable. I don't want to interfere, but she idolizes you. She's pretty, bright, honest, capable, what more do you want?" Could he tell her, "Mom, if she touches me I want to scream; if I see her nude nothing happens"? Mother was right, but what's in these dreams prevents it. Could he tell his mother about them? No! The other day it occurred to him, maybe he and I just couldn't get together, we weren't on the same wave length. There was nothing wrong with me, he wanted me to know that, but maybe he needed a different doctor. Maybe with a different analyst—was he blaming it on me? I, as his father; he wanting to get off the couch to strike. . . .

Don's dramatic style made me wonder how much genuine ego integration and synthesis was actually taking place. A dream representing his hostility in terms of people rather than monsters and shrikes[3] and containing signs of a more constructively operating superego, suggested that progress had been made. My intervention made it possible for him to see his rage in its oedipal context. My refusal to grant him absolution for his self-absorption did not improve his temper but did require him to accept responsibility for his hostility and examine it more carefully. In analytic terms, I could observe a change in intersystemic dynamics: confrontation between ego and superego was superceding that between ego and id. Homosexuality, aggression, and orality were all present in the dreams, but only in the background. His associations made plain that at the center of the stage was his wish for a new object with whom he could identify.

More than a year later, Don J., still acting out, still appalled by the licentiousness of the times, dreamed:

[3] See dreams, "Monster squirts urine" (p. 139) and "Rude in hotel room, then sorry" (p. 234).

I am about to conduct an orchestra. The music can't be found. I look all about for the master score from which all the other parts must be copied and on which all depends. I get desperate. Where is it? I can't find it.

The night before, a young woman had come to his apartment, ostensibly on business. As she was leaving, he embraced her and within a short time had her performing fellatio. Worst of all was that he did not want to tell me about it. That dream—he needed the score to guide him.

I intervened: "The score, which is responsible for all the rest, was not there. Last night you were irresponsible, without the proper score."

After a long silence, "It was no good. I should have had better sense." Then, after further silent reflection, he burst into tears and berated himself at some length for his past conduct.

Dreams that tell of being unprepared, of being unable to move or to complete a task, are related to Freud's "examination dream" (1900) in the sense of containing self-reproaches; they merely lack the consoling aspect of the latter, one that Freud specifically attributed to the "waking agency" (p. 274). Such dreams of failure convey the sense of something improperly done. Together with the distinctly apprehensive affect, they confirm the presence of the superego in their formation. The failure is the failure of not living up to a mandate. Experience validates Freud's somewhat tentative explanation of the latent content of examination dreams: that they refer to being " 'stupid' and 'childish' in . . . the repetition of reprehensible sexual acts" (p. 276).

Toward the end of his analysis, Paul D. brought a singularly terse dream which reflected the stock-taking going on within himself.

Out of a wooded place came a pig with bristles all over.

For the first time in a long while, he somehow felt less irritable with me.... Money, money, money.... Last night he gave a hat-check girl a quarter to retrieve two coats. She demanded two quarters, one for each coat. At first he was incensed, then thought, "Ah, why be a stingy bastard, I can afford it and she needs it." The prospect of a better-paying job had come up, and he decided to discuss this and other financial matters with his wife instead of excluding her as he usually did.... He was beginning to realize as never before that, for all his good manners, he was "a very hostile type," even with me.

While the dream condensed a host of ideas that included sexual aggression and guilt, nothing in the context or associations warranted an interpretation on that level. Paul's growing self-awareness was reflected in the dream: his superego recognized and would no longer give way to that other aspect of himself, the dirty selfish pig who masturbated and had sadomasochistic fantasies.

After ten years of inflicting and accepting torment, Hugo W., as one result of analysis, decided to separate from his wife. In no time at all he took up with a young, glamorous divorcee and, to all appearances, life seemed a whole lot more fun. Only gradually did I discover that Hugo did not find the new lady altogether satisfactory. He neglected to tell me details of the affair, details he preferred not to face.

I told him as much and reminded him of his old habit of remaining oblivious to the obvious. That night he had a dream:

I am at a party—crowded, dingy, a dark place, many people, lots of smoke. I was there alone. People expressed regret at my marital bust-up. An old classmate of mine, X, now very successful and authoritative, spoke to me. He reminded me of you. He shook my hand but looked at me questioningly, quizzically. He was skeptical. I associate that with you, too.

X had never liked him, saw through his essential phoniness, but in the dream he did shake hands though he looked quizzical. As he said that, he thought of me. So many people there and it was dark. Funny it should be so dark. "Something you don't want to look at too closely," I said. "Everything was dark and dim except X; he stood out in a sharp light." . . . Last evening he went to his girl's place for dinner. Right after he got there he began to feel faint, nauseous, perspiring. He told her he didn't feel well. She said he didn't look well and suggested he go home, which he did. He had a little chest pain—maybe he'd been smoking too much? The room in the dream had been smoky. He went to bed right away and evidently slept it off because he woke up early, right after the dream. He started to think about the girl. How callous of her to suggest he go home when he felt so rotten. Yet maybe she was right; when you feel that way it's best to be alone. On the other hand, he might have passed out.

"Yesterday I called into question your relationship with this girl."

"That's true. You were skeptical, quizzical, as in the

dream. I never liked that man, though I wanted his respect and affection. He was always so contemptuous of people; he manipulated them."

"You are really talking about me. You didn't want to hear what I said yesterday. I shouldn't ask you questions."

Hugo fled to another subject, but I brought him back. "You do it again. You don't want to talk about the girl. In effect you are telling me to leave you alone."

"But I don't come here to be left alone." (I considered this a step forward.[4])

"In your dream you were alone and people were talking to you about the divorce. *You* could be skeptical about what you are doing."

"Yes. Did I do right, separating from my wife? And did I handle things right when we were married? I never shared things with her, and now I'm doing the same thing with this new girl—sometimes I have nothing to say to her."

Hugo's dream contained his reaction to my intervention of the day before. He picked up my quizzicality because he had to question himself. His defensive ego denied reality; his observing ego would no longer tolerate the denial exposed by interpretation. Before I could call attention to the dream's reference to his self-criticism, his failure to accept the evidence of his experience with the lady, I had to deal with resistance. I could then make clear what he denied, what he saw but would not look at.

Were we to plot a graph of activity for any analysis, the result would probably show a series of sharp peaks and

---

[4] See dream, "Pushed parked car" (p. 71).

valleys interspersed with long plateaus. These last, representative of the psychoanalyst's dog-days, would consume most of the space, but it would be incorrect to interpret them as registering a total absence of analytic development. In fact, these plateaus can be concerned as much with the patient's internal processes of growth, integration, and intrapsychic realignment as with resistance. Such periods of reorganization are not fallow. They are constructive intervals and provide a moratorium allowing for the build-up of forces which lead to renewed activity. So it is with dreams.

For three months, John Y. went over the same ground he had so often covered before—the same acting out, the same complaints that analysis wasn't doing him any good. During this time he either reported no dreams or ones I could not understand. One Monday he started as usual by dismissing the weekend. Nothing had happened, only this dream:

> I am at a railroad station. A train is pulling in. I just stand and watch it; then I realize it's mine; I'm supposed to be on it. I wonder if I will make it. I left my bags back in the car. I got back to the car, thinking, "Now do everything right, don't mess it up." There is a little blue bag and a felt hat. I think, "What do I need a felt hat for, to go to Washington?" Then I see my father and I'm surprised. He wasn't around before. He just says, "Coming?" He doesn't seem urgent or reproving, merely matter-of-fact and rather kind. It seems as though I might be able to make it.

He thought perhaps his father stood for me, but that was unlikely because I was not so kind. His father said, "Coming?" He had a date Friday night but it came to nothing.

241

On Saturday he saw one of his old girl friends. She masturbated him. There was a kid's song, "Hold on, I'm coming," he thought very funny because of its double entendre. . . . Washington made him think of the father of his country. Missing the train made him think of missing something critical. He couldn't remember his father appearing as himself in a dream before. That was strange. Then too, his father had not been impatient or critical—just reminding him (the quiet but powerful voice of the superego-analyst). "Goddamit, there are plenty of specific things in that dream but. . . . [He was obviously waiting for me to intervene but I did not.] My father, just waiting there, reminded me of you."

"Waiting, while you fool around with the bags," I said.

After a long pause he said, with rare depth of feeling, "I know. I'm not defending my actions this weekend. I'm going to miss the train if I don't stop fooling around. My father's 'Coming?' had to do with more than just missing a train. I know how little sense it makes to go out with girls. Even my repartee makes me sick and tired. I know I like to argue with you, but you don't argue back with me. And I go on playing this waste-of-time game, telling you to go to hell, even though you don't say anything. That blue bag was cheap, like the way I've been behaving."

The next day John offered a postscript. He was impressed by his confrontation with himself as brought out in the dream. He thought my interpretation had been a reproach, as if I had told him to have nothing to do with girls. But the dream was his own, so where was the evidence for imputing such a reproach to me?

The growth of his powers of discernment will be evident if this dream is compared with two of John's other dreams which occurred four and sixteen months earlier.[5] Resistance still operated, but his dream and his reaction to it indicated he was beginning to find a place in his life for a constructive superego. My intervention was calculated to reinforce this process.

John's ego capacity for objective observation had been so corrupted that years had to be spent restoring it to function. His hitherto ubiquitous refrain, "What does it have to do with me?" employed to deny responsibility for actions dictated by his unconscious, had to be interpreted repeatedly as a defense if everything else were not to remain unconvincing to him.

John's hypothetical graph continued to show expectable ups and downs. Then, after the summer recess, I noticed that for the first time he was arriving five minutes early instead of appearing on the stroke of the hour. His depressions were shallower, his masturbation less frequent, his acting out in casual affairs gave him less and less satisfaction. He complained that everything seemed to have come to a standstill; he was in a state of suspended animation and felt strange. Everything was different and yet it wasn't. In this context, five months after the last dream given, he brought this one:

> I was here, waking up as though I had been asleep, fainted or paralyzed and just realized where I was— disoriented, a very funny feeling. I was lying on the couch, like now. More passed out than asleep. I said out loud, "God, where am I, what happened?" It felt very significant [am I figuring it out?]. You said, in a clini-

---

[5] Respectively, "Sleeping bags recede" (p. 199) and "Late to analyst's office— wrong street" (p. 78).

cal manner, without concern, "How do your arms feel?" Then you reached over and touched my arm. I said, "I can't move." It seemed to be the end of the hour. I got up and saw two pairs of shoes on the floor. I put one pair on, walked out, saw it was the wrong pair, came back and knocked to say I had taken the wrong ones.

He saw no connection with anything that happened yesterday. He thought of asking me what I made of it. Such a very definite dream, the most definite he'd had in a long time. Like he actually passed out because he got too close to something—a very funny feeling.... His arm was paralyzed sounded antimasturbatory, but that was pure generalizing crap. Why last night? Yesterday he did a lighting job for a show. Saturday night, at a party, he kissed a girl. It felt good, but was mechanical, no contact, a losing game but not quite the same game. Paralyzed, not doing anything, reminded him of something I'd said: "Can't do something on my father's land" (a reference to an interpretation to a dream of a week before: "Nothing can happen in father's territory"). The big thing in this dream was his being paralyzed; it seemed so significant.... Yesterday, working with the lights, he had to insert fuses.... "Like if you put your prick in you get a shock." What had all this to do with the dream?

Here I felt it incumbent upon me to say, as I had many times before, "Still figuring it out?"

Yes, he was. Wasn't that what he was here for? He would be glad to hear from me what the dream had to do with. He realized he was being defensive, maybe offensive.... It was useless to try to figure it out, only made things worse; he did it all the time. He would like to relax; if he could relax maybe he wouldn't have to be here. Faking a "smartass pose." (He reviewed the dream again and expressed annoyance at not being able to "figure it out." When I refused his bait, he continued.)

"There ought to be a school where they would teach you to feel something, to think instead of talking all the time. . . ." He felt shut off, no relation to me, just a string of words (I considered this insight). Acting out but not feeling anything. . . . Yesterday his son called him and, "sonof-agun, if it wasn't like having a friend. Imagine. He liked me. It was a funny feeling. Somebody considers me necessary."

Just as a manifest dream depicting incest must not be taken at face value, so one presenting apparent homosexual overtures has to be read in its clinical context. My *touching* him was not a sexual act, but a visual metaphor related to his growing involvement with analysis and identification with the analyst. *Waking up* could be regarded as the equivalent of his newly gained insight. The poignant plea for "feeling," to be touched in the manifest dream, was expressed in his associations after I had interpreted his resistance. In the wake of the dissolution of his defenses, John found himself bewildered, disoriented, in limbo, paralyzed by his inability to act out as formerly. The dream registered and reported all this through the agency of an awakened ego.

This dream and hour were the result of years of un-remitting analysis of and meticulous attention to resistance and defenses, reinforcing my conviction that the analytic process was transforming an intellectual exercise into a living experience.

I wish I knew what the "shoes" were doing in the dream. It would be tempting to substitute "women" for shoes and to interpret John's return of them to their rightful owner as a rendering unto Caesar (and father) what is his. I am afraid we have no warrant. Shoes might also be shoes or something else demanding a whole chain of thought for its understanding. May I say it again? If we interpret out of context, without associations, we play a game and an unconvincing one at that.

Childhood's cherished fantasies die hard. In the course of analysis, Simon E. resisted every deflation of the fantasy that the world was his for the asking. His attitude toward the need to make a living and support his family slowly evolved from an outrageous imposition, to a burden he could not avoid, to a challenge he struggled to meet. The childhood wish for success changed its aim and bore the imprint of a determination to be as good as other men. Nevertheless, from time to time Simon sighed for his mythical Garden of Eden which, in more rational moments, he knew no longer existed. While preparing to meet a new assignment which called for prolonged and intense study, he had this dream:

> I was back at school. Everything was different. The buildings were changed, more modern. I saw new boys walking around whom I did not know. I felt left out. I looked about and wondered what it was like here now.

From the way he told the dream, I knew its affect was not depressive, but to make sure, I asked, "What was your feeling?"

"I wasn't sad, just felt everything was different. It's hard to explain."

His associations dwelt on his increasing ability to cope

with situations in various areas. The dream made him think of Thomas Wolfe's *Look Homeward Angel* and *You Can't Go Home Again.* It made him feel more regretful than distressed.

To fortify these encouraging developments, I said, "It isn't the way it used to be with you. *You* have changed." His voice brightened. "I feel older. It's different all right. I'm not sure I like it. Something is passing, has passed. It seems a pity."

I could not help contrasting this dream with some of his earlier ones.[6] The same oral craving underlay them all—but with what a difference.

Analysis is a backward-and-forward process. In the dream, as in symptoms and general behavior, there is always a compromise between regressive and progressive functioning. Ordinarily, the presentation of my bill was enough to send Simon into waves of resentment, succeeded by prolonged sulking. A few months after the hour just described and following receipt of my bill, he dreamed of coming to my office and finding another psychiatrist there who told him I had died of a heart attack. Even though the dream added to his tension, I did not interpret it. I preferred to let him face its implications and give him time to extend them. I could afford to do this the more easily because of our reliable working alliance. I knew, despite the anguish his rage and aggression were generating, that he had advanced to the point where he could tolerate their expression, particularly in the transference.

Two days later he came in, handed me a check, and said

---

[6] See dreams, "Excluded in country bedroom" (pp. 114-115) and "Rejected for not working" (p. 116).

cheerfully, "I feel much better today." Then he told me two dreams.

> I was moving into the business at the family store. My brother was there wearing a gay-nineties' moustache, its apparent effect being to make me afraid. I turned on him in fury and said, "*You* make *me* afraid? Never again."

> Then I was driving with someone—I don't know who— he was sitting in the back. Up ahead was a lady. At an intersection where construction was going on, she tried to beat me out. At first I got angry, "I'll show her." Then I thought, "Ah, what are you getting all excited about? Let her go, it's her problem," and I cooled off.

He had come home tired, resisted a temptation to rest, to "goof off," and instead sat down and paid all his bills. He had an attack of diarrhea afterward, though. The moustache was like one his son put on for Halloween. When he turned on his brother, he felt as if he were putting "paid" to all the insults he had ever suffered at his hands—there would be no more of that. Strange to say, he was actually getting along better with his brother now than he had for years. . . . He was feeling better about himself these days, more responsible. . . . He supposed having to make out a check and give me money made him angry as it usually did, made him want to say, "This is it, I've had enough," as he did to his brother. . . . That construction area in the dream—an addition was going up at the family store.

"You are being more constructive," I said, "you are not letting things get you so much."

He paused while scrutinizing this for hidden bombs, as though he were wondering if it were possible for people to like him when he hated them so much. Then—yes, he had noticed a marked change in his mood from yesterday. He realized the extent of his "silent stewing." It wasn't easy, but he could move around a little bit more now than he used to, wasn't so depressed. He remembered at the start of analysis how angry he got when cars passed him. He had to overtake them. He could be calmer about that now. But he just knew writing that check would cause hell. He could feel a difference, but he still got the diarrhea. Although he felt better about himself, the ground was still shaky, like the construction area filled with loose boards (an added detail). In the dream he didn't think he would get through it but he did.

In Simon's dream, "driving with someone—I don't know who . . . in the back," clearly referred to me, but in light of the trend of his associations I saw no need to spell it out. Enough that the dream said and his associations confirmed that he was actively engaged in reconciling the conflict of interests between rage and reason.

As the analytic process lifts repression, as unconscious libidinal and aggressive impulses are restored to awareness, the mode of dream work changes in accordance with the alteration in the ego's mechanisms of defense. No longer does the dream have to resort to old means of representation or symbolic substitutes for inadmissible drive representations. The ego's enhanced functions of synthesis and integration allow new methods of accommodation and adaptation for ancient, infantile appetites. This may be reflected in, and even anticipated by, the dream's altered manifest appearance.

For several months after the beginning of his analysis, Roy L. recurrently dreamed of flying, either unaided or, as time went on, with the assistance of powerful aeronautical devices. Such dreams were accompanied by feelings of euphoria and elation reflecting his narcissism and primitive evaluation of erectile potency. While skyborne in his dreams, he exhibited a lofty, overbearing attitude in his behavior both in and outside analysis. As the latter proceeded, producing anger and frustration with depression in their train, so his dreams came down to earth. The elation and triumph of these nighttime aerial adventures yielded to anxiety as his planes crashed or he was brought low from his unaided solo flights. Eventually, the flying dreams receded, then, with the development of transference as well as with the improvement in his object relations, disappeared altogether.

The drives, of course, are immortal. In moments of weakness or stress, in severe illness or conflict, when the ego and its bodily substratum are threatened, they may reassert themselves. Delirium, upsetting the balance of regulatory forces, may instate anew our earlier methods of mentation and bring back the old dreams.

As a consequence of the analysis of defenses erected to forestall the emergence of anxiety they provoke, aggressive impulses, expressed in rage and anger, inevitably come to the fore, not least in dreams. John Y., for instance, dreamed, to begin with, of ominous storm clouds gathering in and gradually covering the sky, or of violent explosions, of scenes of carnage, of landscapes laid waste. With diminution of anxiety, aided by analytic support and growth of his ego functions of observation, accommodation, and integration, and with reduction of superego retaliation, such dreams gradually subsided and changed character. That they did not totally disappear can be attributed to either the strength of these impulses, insufficient containment by identification with an adequately "good" parent or parents, or to the limitations of analysis. Nevertheless, whatever change did take place in intersystemic alignment was reflected in dreams that indicated modulation of primitive aggression, that presented it in terms of self-assertive confrontations in his object relations, rather than by archaic images of destruction.

Testifying to changes in superego functioning, the policeman who so often makes an appearance in dreams as a manifestation of its punitive presence yields to more kindly surrogates in the form of self-directed admonitions or remorseful reproaches. Simon E.'s "Ah.... Let her go," in the dream just cited, reflected a tempering of his rage against his mother for being faithless, but was as well a self-release, to be read, "I, too, can be let go"—from the bondage he experienced in his family.

Dreaming is a fundamental, organismic function. Analysis may bring it out, but it cannot create it. For many people, it begins the process of analysis and ends it, as though the dream were a preferred method of discourse with themselves. What we might call a trait, evinced in this way, continues in evidence throughout their lives, including their analytic life and experience. It may be that a certain kind of creativity comes to the fore and is attached to dreaming, a capacity that by itself offers no guarantee of mind expansion; only informed application to it can result in enhanced self-awareness. Don J., for instance, generally acknowledged as superior in his chosen field of artistic endeavor, continued to be a prolific dreamer even in periods of resistance. His dreams not only did not dwindle then, they came forward in profusion to give voice to resistance to the analytic process embodied in defenses he had difficulty in giving up.

There are those whose limitations extend, beyond anything analysis can do, to psychic impoverishment, including their dream life. Paul D. maintained his characterological parsimoniousness in sparse dream contributions throughout analysis. The anal manifestations of obsessive-compulsive withholding, fear of affect, intense need for control had become a way of life that could no longer be altered. In consequence, his capacity for creativity, for new solutions, for dreaming, remained limited, as the goals of analysis had to be. He had no talent, no taste for the creative regression dreams make possible. One must, after all, make allowances for preferred modes of thinking, as for tastes.

13

Countertransference
in Dreams

Coming full cycle after an interval of several years, I return
to expand on remarks made in the introduction to this book.
It was noted there that the dream seems to have fallen into
disuse; that analytic training may not provide analysts with
the conviction that comes from experiencing their own
dreams; that those recently trained in psychoanalysis do not
know what to do with the dream.

This chapter is concerned with the second of these statements, although all three are intimately related. It is
addressed to the analyst's experience of his own dreams and
to the value of this experience in deepening and broadening
analytic acuity.

The motives an analyst has for dreaming, recalling his
dreams, and working with them are not exhausted when he
terminates his own analysis. Apart from the help his dreams
may offer him in illuminating personal problems, it is

essential that he have recourse to them for the sharpening of his therapeutic instrument—the intimate knowledge and understanding of the workings of his own unconscious. Insofar as these bear on the work he does with his patients, his reactions, whether in the area of countertransference or as responses to the real aspects of the doctor-patient relation, are crucial elements in his work.

Writing about his treatment of Emmy von N., Freud remarked, "In the first quarter of an hour after waking I remembered all the dreams I had had during the night, and I took the trouble to write them down and try to solve them" (Breuer and Freud, 1893-1895, p. 69n). And a number of years later he said, "If I am asked how one can become a psycho-analyst, I reply: 'By studying one's own dreams'" (1910, p. 33). These injunctions may have been neglected in the intervening time, but I do not believe they have ever been challenged.

Freud's sharing of his dreams with the world was, at the time, a practical necessity in explicating his discoveries about the interpretation of dreams: for the most part, he had only his own to work with. Even if we no longer operate under the same necessity, our own dreams are indispensable to us as extensions of our professional apparatus. We do not hear very much about this aspect of the analyst's activities. I have found it eminently worthwhile to share certain dreams with colleagues and students, for teaching purposes, and have myself profited from what I learned in return. Of course the reader would not thank me for serving up, if that were indeed possible, a sampler of my psyche as revealed by my dreams. I shall confine myself to presenting a few dreams that deal with countertransference reactions.

Analysis is, after all, an interpersonal transaction, not a

bloodless affair, and analysts must react to their patients. To react *to*, however, is not to react *with*, and it becomes mandatory that the analyst know what he is reacting to in order that he not react with. Certainly nobody would claim that the analyst, no matter how well analyzed, lives in a therapeutic vacuum excluding all libidinal and aggressive cathexes of his or her patients. Even if such a state were attainable, its desirability is arguable, for we should only have succeeded in supplying the patient with a dehumanized analyst, and no analysis would be possible. What we require is that the analyst recognize, control, and use to good effect, in the patient's interest, the responses the patient generates in him.

A middle-aged lady with three children did not stir me to any conscious fantasies of amatory conquest or admiration for her feminine charms. She had persevered in a lengthy analysis that had enabled her to overcome a good many of her oedipal and preoedipal conflicts, marry, and raise a family. Now she was struggling to free herself from residual transference attachments as the analysis was approaching termination. In this setting, saturated with separation anxiety, she reverted expectably to fantasies of reunion with the lost objects of childhood, became disenchanted with her husband and present family life, and dreamed profusely of new romantic attachments. The analytic atmosphere was charged with her longing, her sorrow that she could not retain the analyst for the fulfillment of her heart's desire. Explicit in this context was the expression of her wish for physical contact, denied her by her husband, who seemed overwhelmed by her demands for sexual satisfaction.

From time to time, I felt compassion for her: poor lady,

she was being spurned on all sides. Something about my responses alerted me to the possibility that I was involved in a way that required as much scrutiny of myself as of the patient, especially when I was visited by a series of dreams. They began innocently enough, or so it appeared.

> I was in an apartment with the patient. She first in-
> dicated to me a large table spread with an assortment
> of sweets. Next she offered me melons and other fruits.
> Finally she presented me with a bunch of flowers.

I was not disconcerted. I could recognize the sexual significance concealed by the symbols of sweets and fruits and flowers, but resistance was doing its work and de-priving this recognition of any affective meaning. So far, it was merely an "interesting" dream. This ingenuousness was not to last. When the dream work seemed to put aside its disguises and a subsequent dream frankly offered up the patient as a sexual partner, the waking and remembering analyst had also to give up his denial and admit the obvious.

How to integrate this information with my working day? It may be that if a countertransference manifestation such as this does not reach the analyst's awareness, he will respond with his customary defenses, or even, by acting out. In either case, the analytic process is put in jeopardy. An opportunity for investigating the patient's line of de-velopment in object relations, in the genesis and vicissitudes of libidinal and aggressive fantasies associated with them, is lost. The analyst's resistances make common cause with those of the patient. If transference, indispensable as it is, can become the ground for resistance, countertransference serves equally well to impede the progress of analysis. Here especially, if attended to, the analyst's dreams are his ally as they reflect and reveal the unconscious aspects of his own libidinal (or aggressive) object relations. In this case, the analyst had to come to terms with rescue fantasies from childhood, dormant oedipal temptations, and with his own separation anxiety, which the analytic situation brought to life for him as well as for the patient.

The following illustrates another way the analyst's dream helps him in his work.

My office is in a dismal state of disarray. The painters have been there and left their gear all about. Chairs are not in their accustomed places and are obstructing traffic. The bell won't work. I can't get ready. Patients are about to arrive, and I am getting anxious. When and how will I be able to see them?[1]

This dream recurs from time to time, with variations on the theme. The anxiety is familiar, a reminder of conflict about doing one's duty. How odd, or perhaps not so odd, that, even so, resistance operates each time to prevent me from admitting I would rather not see or listen to that early-in-the morning patient who has been injuring my pride by calling my competence into question. The dream's recurrence bespeaks an ongoing conflict that requires solution. In the manifest dream, my office was being systematically rendered unfit for service. The surface of the dream represents a complaint. The patient who evoked it was a walking compendium of complaints, reproaches, and rebukes, daily reducing me to rubble. The dream intro-

[1] Compare with dreams, "Busy doctor has no time" (p. 78) and "Late to analyst's office—wrong street" (p. 78).

duces me as a consortium of painters whose disorderly activity deprives me of my working arrangements. The patient is not doing the work he should be doing; I counter with a mirror image of his disruptiveness. If he is engaged in a battle for narcissistic supremacy, I shall outdo him. I defeat myself before he can defeat me.

Such is what the dream tells me; knowing it, am I better off? Yes, if it teaches me not to oppose my will to his, to let him do the only thing possible—re-enact his infantile omnipotence.

Years ago, when I was starting to practice and was concerned about getting patients, I was grateful to have a young man referred to me for help. I was in the middle of my analytic training and saw him for psychotherapy, which he, to my dismay, insisted was analysis, despite his sitting face to face with me. I felt uneasy, unsure of my ability, anxious that he not find me wanting or discover that I was groping with what I knew to be meager and insufficient equipment. I certainly did not want to lose a patient I sorely needed.

The patient said he was troubled by his lack of friends, fear of women, masturbation, and vague homosexual stirrings which he had never acted upon. He expressed his willingness to be most cooperative and tell me anything I wanted to know. Thereafter, to my consternation, he remained silent, protesting that he could not say anything without my asking him questions. After a few painful sessions with him, I dreamed:

I am having a homosexual affair with Mr. X. (the patient). It is not clear who is the active one and who is

passive. But how is it to be done? Fellatio? Per anus?
I am attracted and yet horrified, and wake up as from
a nightmare in great anxiety.

My first reaction was an impulse to get away from the
manifest implications of the dream; my second was to
wonder whether I was indeed homosexual and, if so, why
hadn't anybody ever told me. It was only years later that I
could understand what was at issue.

Just as the meaning of symptoms and the genesis of a
neurosis become clear only after years of work and intense
concentration, so the meaning of a dream may become
apparent only after the passage of considerable time,
perhaps at the end of analysis, or long after. Connections or
solutions can occur at the oddest moments—and probably
will, if one is receptive to what dreams have to offer.

In preparing this chapter, that dream of long ago came to
mind. I had wanted very much to understand and help the
patient, but how could I when he was not telling me what I
needed to know? The manifest dream portrays a mutual
endeavor conducted on an intimate level in sexual terms.
The dream presents me as functional—I was at least
capable of performing sexually—even if it still posed the
problem of how the function was to be performed. One
might call this a dream of convenience: "If you don't know
what else to do, you can at least do this." My relation with
the patient was not comfortable, and I was trying to
redeem it. A sexual relation, wordless though it might be,
was better than none at all. It was a way of binding him to
me, albeit in dream language, on a regressive level of
discourse. My dream, in effect, attempted to solve the
problem of communication with the patient.

Such a bald presentation of homosexuality with attendant anxiety concealed deeper levels of aggression toward the patient, born of frustration, from which the anxiety more truly stems. Significant deeper determinants for the dream concerned estrangement from an important figure in the past: the longing for reunion with this lost object, confusion over who was responsible for the separation, and what I could do about it. But this insight notwithstanding, the interpretation "upward," on a level apposite to the current therapeutic relation between doctor and patient, would have been most helpful to me, had I been able to make it at the time.

A married professional woman came for help because of marital discord, abhorrence of her husband's sexual advances, disaffection with and rage at her young son, and depression. Although past thirty, her stance was more that of a teenager. Her behavior in psychotherapy quickly approximated this developmental stage. She lost herself in reveries when with me, asked to know the details of my family life and my preferences in hobbies, professed daydreaming about me in the intervals between visits, hoped that I reciprocated by thinking about her, and even wondered aloud why a psychiatrist could not see his patients outside the office, over a drink perhaps.

These florid expressions of her regard alternated with savage denunciations. She hated me for my callous indifference, my preference for my other patients; she accused me of wanting to be rid of her; she wished she were dead.

Even in her better moods, she demanded various sorts of special consideration. I complied with her requests for the opening and closing of windows, for a glass of water, but not with her demands for changes in appointment time or reduction of the fee. Her periodically holding up to view the possibility that she would kill herself—she indeed courted disaster by speeding and disregarding traffic signals —or consult another doctor who would solve her problems more efficaciously than I could, made me wonder whether she might actually succeed in acting out something drastic. Would she overdo the ingestion of the tranquillizers she was using to such excess?

In the context of this intense transference atmosphere, I dreamed:

> I was at home with my wife and the patient. All of us were relaxed and amiable. I was glad she was with the family. It was a pleasant situation.

To do a good job—everything was so good in the dream—recurred insistently as part of my response to the dream. In what is manifest, I seem to have put a stop to the turbulent treatment situation, eliminated all ambivalence —hers and mine—and made her a gift of membership in my family. The dream seems to be a stunning wish-fulfillment—all hands satisfied. I have been admirably magnanimous to the patient in thus admitting her, as she clearly wanted, to intimacy with me and mine—with one exception: for her to be happily together with my wife was utterly at variance with her vehemently expressed wishes. She had made it abundantly clear that she viewed my wife's existence as both superfluous and undesirable. So I was not being agreeable after all, but, in fact, rather unpleasant. The dream was no longer so good to everybody.

Then why this—by now patently false—accommodation? To whom was the dream so "good," and why? Even though I could readily understand the patient's threats to leave me for a more satisfactory therapist who would provide her with surcease from sorrow better than I could, I was nevertheless irritated. And, in replacing disaffection with affection (see Freud's dream of the uncle with the yellow beard [1900, p. 137]) I was working too hard to have "everything nice." Such a façade reflected my attempts to appease the patient with what can only properly be called therapeutic zeal, an investment of effort that exhausts the analyst and does the patient no good. The manifest dream was calculated to conceal my quite opposite feelings for the patient, which made her presence far from relaxing or pleasant. My ambivalence about her was the mirror image of her oscillations between love and hate for me.

The reflections stimulated by the dream made it possible to regard my relations with the patient in the treatment situation with more detachment. They helped me to regain a good measure of confidence about what I was doing with her. Integration of feelings from the past with those of the present relieved conflict and, with its subsidence, brought renewed interest and understanding of the patient's problems and of what she must go through to achieve the same end. Analysis of the dream enabled me to accept her level of functioning with more equanimity.

The patient's presence in the dream had other determinants; she stood as surrogate for someone other than herself. Moreover, the dream expressed deeper wishes of my own for restitution of losses suffered. My purpose here, however, has been to call attention to the need for close examination of the therapeutic relationship when a patient figures in the analyst's dreams.

The analyst, like everyone else, loves and hates. He may become depressed, may even have a spell of paranoia. He will, from time to time, catch himself being masochistic and indeed, with that, sadistic. Nor can he avoid being overtaken by anxiety when threatened from without or within. He will hesitate, doubt, seek reassurance when ambivalence upsets his balance. What is required is that he know what steps to take to trace his reactions to their source and correct them. The analyst's dreams, if he will grant them a place in his mental economy—his mental housekeeping—will come to his aid in this regard as will nothing else.

*   *   *

In bringing this book to a close, I would like to emphasize, at the risk of stating the obvious, that for didactic purposes I have used as illustrations only those dreams I could work with. I realize that reading one after the other as I have presented them could well be misleading if the idea were conveyed that I invariably understood or interpreted every dream reported, or that I spent the greater part of the time with dreams. Let it be clearly understood that the dreams which eluded me far outnumbered those I could bring into the analytic process.

One final word: psychoanalysis is of course involved with a great deal more than the interpretation of dreams. But we cannot hope to help our patients know themselves in depth unless we take that most extraordinary road to the unconscious—unless, understanding its limitations as well as its possibilities, we make the dream an essential part of psychoanalysis.

Bibliography

REFERENCES

Baudry, F. (1974), Remarks on Spoken Words in Dreams. *Psychoanal. Quart.*, 43:581-605.

Breuer, J. & Freud, S. (1893-1895), Studies on Hysteria. *Standard Edition*, 2:69n. London: Hogarth Press, 1955.

Fisher, C. (1965), Psychoanalytic Implications of Recent Research on Sleep and Dreaming. *J. Amer. Psychoanal. Assn.*, 13:197-303.

Freud, S. (1900), The Interpretation of Dreams. *Standard Edition*, 4 & 5. London: Hogarth Press, 1953.

_____(1905), Fragment of an Analysis of a Case of Hysteria. *Standard Edition*, 7:3-122. London: Hogarth Press, 1953.

_____(1910), Five Lectures on Psycho-Analysis. *Standard Edition*, 11:33-37. London: Hogarth Press, 1957.

_____(1916), Introductory Lectures on Psycho-Analysis. *Standard Edition*, 15. London: Hogarth Press, 1963.

Isakower, O. (1938), A Contribution to the Patho-Psychology of Phenomena Associated with Falling Asleep. *Internat. J. Psycho-Anal.*, 19:331-345.

_____(1954), Spoken Words in Dreams. *Psychoanal. Quart.*, 23:1-6.

Lewin, B. D. (1946), Sleep, the Mouth and the Dream Screen. *Psychoanal. Quart.*, 15:419-434.

BIBLIOGRAPHY

_____(1948a), Inferences from the Dream Screen. *Internat. J. Psycho-Anal.*, 29:224-231.
_____(1948b), The Nature of Reality, the Meaning of Nothing, with an Addendum on Concentration. *Psychoanal. Quart.*, 17:524-526.
_____(1953), Reconsiderations of the Dream Screen. *Psychoanal. Quart.*, 22:174-199.
Rosenbaum, M. (1965), Dreams in Which the Analyst Appears Undisguised, a Clinical and Statistical Study. *Internat. J. Psycho-Anal.*, 46:429-437.

BASIC READINGS[1]

Freud, S. (1900), The Interpretation of Dreams. *Standard Edition*, 4 & 5. London: Hogarth Press, 1953.
_____(1901), On Dreams. *Standard Edition*, 5:629-686. London: Hogarth Press, 1953.
_____(1905), Fragment of an Analysis of a Case of Hysteria. *Standard Edition*, 7:3-122. London: Hogarth Press, 1953.
_____(1909), Notes upon a Case of Obsessional Neurosis. *Standard Edition*, 10:192-193, 218n. London: Hogarth Press, 1955.
_____(1910), Five Lectures on Psycho-Analysis. *Standard Edition*, 11:33-37. London: Hogarth Press, 1957.
_____(1911), On the Handling of Dream-Interpretation in Psycho-Analysis. *Standard Edition*, 12:91-96. London: Hogarth Press, 1958.
_____(1913), An Evidential Dream. *Standard Edition*, 12:269-277. London: Hogarth Press, 1958.
_____(1916), Introductory Lectures on Psycho-Analysis. *Standard Edition*, 15:83-239. London: Hogarth Press, 1963.
_____(1917), A Metapsychological Supplement to the Theory of Dreams. *Standard Edition*, 14:219-235. London: Hogarth Press, 1957.
_____(1918), From the History of an Infantile Neurosis. *Standard Edition*, 17:5-122. London: Hogarth Press, 1955.
_____(1923), Remarks on the Theory and Practice of Dream-Interpretation. *Standard Edition*, 19:109-121. London: Hogarth Press, 1961.

[1] *Author's note:* In the interest of readability, I have refrained from burdening the text with attributions. A book on the dream in analysis must inevitably find its fundamental sources in Freud. I therefore append here a basic list of his writings on the dream.

_____(1925), Some Additional Notes on Dream-Interpretation as a Whole. *Standard Edition*, 19:127-138. London: Hogarth Press, 1961.

_____(1933), New Introductory Lectures on Psycho-Analysis. *Standard Edition*, 22:7-30. London: Hogarth Press, 1964.

SELECTED SUPPLEMENTARY READINGS

Alexander, F. (1925), Dreams in Pairs and Series. *Internat. J. Psycho-Anal.*, 6:446-452.

Altman, L. L. (1959), West as a Symbol of Death. *Psychoanal. Quart.*, 28:236-241.

Arlow, J. A. (1955), Notes on Oral Symbolism. *Psychoanal. Quart.*, 24:1-63.

_____(1961), A Typical Dream. *J. Hillside Hosp.*, 10:54-58.

Bartemeier, L. H. (1950), Illness Following Dreams. *Internat. J. Psycho-Anal.*, 31:8-10.

Baudry, F. D. (1967), The First Dream in Analysis. Presentation at Affiliated Staff Meeting, Treatment Center, New York Psychoanalytic Institute.

Bergmann, M. S. (1966), The Intrapsychic and Communicative Aspects of the Dream. *Internat. J. Psycho-Anal.*, 47:356-363.

Blank, H. R. (1958), Dreams of the Blind. *Psychoanal. Quart.*, 27:158-174.

Blitzsten, N. L., Eissler, R. S., & Eissler, K. R. (1950), Emergence of Hidden Ego Tendencies During Dream Analysis. *Internat. J. Psycho-Anal.*, 31:12-17.

Eder, M. D. (1930), Dreams as Resistance. *Internat. J. Psycho-Anal.*, 11:40-47.

Eggan, D. (1952), The Manifest Content of Dreams. *Amer. Anthropol.*, 54:469-484.

Eisenbud, J. (1965), The Hand and the Breast with Special Reference to Obsessional Neurosis. *Psychoanal. Quart.*, 34:219-248.

Eisenstein, V. W. (1949), Dreams After Intercourse. *Psychoanal. Quart.*, 18:154-172.

Erikson, E. H. (1954), The Dream Specimen of Psychoanalysis. *J. Amer. Psychoanal. Assn.*, 2:5-56.

Esman, A. H. (1962), The Dream Screen in an Adolescent. *Psychoanal. Quart.*, 31:250-251.

Federn, P. (1932), Ego Feeling in Dreams. *Psychoanal. Quart.*, 1:511-542.

_____(1934), The Awakening of the Ego in Dreams. *Internat. J. Psycho-Anal.*, 15:296-301.

_____(1944), A Dream under General Anesthesia. *Psychiat. Quart.*, 18:422-438.

Feldman, S. S. (1945), Interpretation of a Typical and Stereotyped Dream Met with Only During Psychoanalysis. *Psychoanal. Quart.*, 14:511-515.

Fenichel, O. (1925), The Appearance in a Dream of a Lost Memory. *Collected Papers, 1st series.* New York: W. W. Norton, 1953, pp. 34-38.

_____(1928), Some Infantile Sexual Theories Not Hitherto Described. *Internat. J. Psycho-Anal.*, 9:346-352.

_____(1929), Analysis of a Dream. *Collected Papers, 1st series.* New York: W. W. Norton, 1953, pp. 160-166.

Ferenczi, S. (1950), *Further Contributions to the Theory and Technique of Psychoanalysis.* London: Hogarth Press, pp. 345-349, 352-361.

Fisher, C. (1954), Dreams and Perception. *J. Amer. Psychoanal. Assn.*, 2:389-445.

_____(1956), Dreams, Images, and Perception. *J. Amer. Psychoanal. Assn.*, 4:5-48.

_____(1957), A Study of the Preliminary Stages of the Construction of Dreams and Images. *J. Amer. Psychoanal. Assn.*, 5:5-60.

Fliess, R. (1953), *The Revival of Interest in the Dream.*[2] New York: International Universities Press.

_____(1973), *Symbol, Dream, and Psychosis.* New York: International Universities Press.

Freud, A. (1922), The Relation of Beating Phantasies to a Daydream. *Internat. J. Psycho-Anal.*, 4:89-102.

Freud, S. (1901), The Psychopathology of Everyday Life.[3] *Standard Edition*, 6:277-278. London: Hogarth Press, 1960.

_____(1905), Jokes and Their Relation to the Unconscious. *Standard Edition*, 8:159-180. London: Hogarth Press, 1960.

_____(1907), Delusions and Dreams in Jensen's *Gradiva. Standard Edition*, 9:7-95. London: Hogarth Press, 1959.

_____(1910), The Antithetical Meaning of Primal Words. *Standard Edition*, 11:155-161. London: Hogarth Press, 1957.

[2] Includes summaries of several articles in this list.

[3] For correspondence of mechanisms of dream formation, symptom, and parapractic formation.

_____(1913a), The Occurrence in Dreams of Material from Fairy Tales. *Standard Edition*, 12:281-287. London: Hogarth Press, 1958.

_____(1913b), The Claims of Psycho-Analysis to Scientific Interest.[4] *Standard Edition*, 13:169-172. London: Hogarth Press, 1955.

_____(1914), On the History of the Psycho-Analytic Movement. *Standard Edition*, 14:7-66. London: Hogarth Press, 1957.

_____(1916), A Connection Between a Symbol and a Symptom. *Standard Edition*, 14:339-340. London: Hogarth Press, 1957.

_____(1920), The Psychogenesis of a Case of Homosexuality in a Woman. *Standard Edition*, 18:164-166. London: Hogarth Press, 1955.

_____(1923a), Two Encyclopaedia Articles.[5] *Standard Edition*, 18:240-242. London: Hogarth Press, 1955.

_____(1923b), A Seventeenth-Century Demonological Neurosis.[6] *Standard Edition*, 19:89. London: Hogarth Press, 1961.

_____(1925), An Autobiographical Study.[7] *Standard Edition*, 20:43-46. London: Hogarth Press, 1959.

_____(1926), Inhibitions, Symptoms and Anxiety. *Standard Edition*, 20:77-175. London: Hogarth Press, 1959.

_____(1929), Some Dreams of Descartes—A Letter to Maxime Leroy. *Standard Edition*, 21:199-204. London: Hogarth Press, 1961.

_____(1932), My Contact with Josef Popper-Lynkeus.[8] *Standard Edition*, 22:219-224. London: Hogarth Press, 1964.

_____(1940), An Outline of Psycho-Analysis.[9] *Standard Edition*, 23:165-171. London: Hogarth Press, 1964.

Friedman, P. (1952), The Bridge: A Study in Symbolism. *Psychoanal. Quart.*, 21:49-80.

Giovacchini, P. L. (1966), Dreams and the Creative Process. *Brit. J. Med. Psychol.*, 39:105-115.

Greenberg, H. H. & Blank, H. R. (1970), Dreams of a Dying Patient. *Brit. J. Med. Psychol.*, 43:355-362.

Greenson, R. R. (1970), The Exceptional Position of the Dream in Psychoanalytic Practice. *Psychoanal. Quart.*, 39:519-549.

[4] One of Freud's admirable summaries of the place of dreams in psychoanalysis.
[5] Another excellent summary of the place of the dream in psychoanalysis.
[6] On the symbolic significance of some numbers.
[7] Another summary of the dream, but with a different emphasis.
[8] An account of how Freud became interested in dreams.
[9] Freud's last and equally interesting summary of dream theory.

———(1973), The Clinical Use of the Dream Early in Analysis. *Bull. Menninger Clinic*, 37:187-192.

Grigg, K. A. (1973), "All Roads Lead to Rome": The Role of the Nursemaid in Freud's Dreams. *J. Amer. Psychoanal. Assn.*, 21:108-126.

Grinstein, A. (1954), The Convertible as a Symbol in Dreams. *J. Amer. Psychoanal. Assn.*, 2:466-472.

Gross, A. (1949), Sense of Time in Dreams. *Psychoanal. Quart.*, 18:466-470.

Grotjahn, M. (1945), Laughter in Dreams. *Psychoanal. Quart.*, 14:221-227.

Harris, I. D. (1960), Typical Anxiety Dreams and Object Relations. *Internat. J. Psycho-Anal.*, 41:604-611.

———(1962), Dreams About the Analyst. *Internat. J. Psycho-Anal.*, 43:151-158.

Isakower, O. (1939), On the Exceptional Position of the Auditory Sphere. *Internat. J. Psycho-Anal.*, 20:340-348.

Jekels, L. & Bergler, E. (1940), Instinct Dualism in Dreams. *Psychoanal. Quart.*, 9:394-414.

Jones, E. (1911a), Some Instances of the Influence of Dreams on Waking Life. *J. Abn. Psychol.*, 6:11-18.

———(1911b), *On the Nightmare*. New York: Grove Press, 1959.

———(1916), The Theory of Symbolism. In: *Papers on Psychoanalysis*. Boston: Beacon Press, 1961, pp. 87-144.

Kanzer, M. (1945), The Therapeutic Use of Dreams Induced by Hypnotic Suggestion. *Psychoanal. Quart.*, 14:313-335.

———(1955), The Communicative Function of the Dream. *Internat. J. Psycho-Anal.*, 36:260-266.

———(1959), The Recollection of the Forgotten Dream. *J. Hillside Hosp.*, 8:74-85.

Knapp, P. H. (1956), Sensory Impressions in Dreams. *Psychoanal. Quart.*, 25:325-347.

Kris, E. (1954), New Contributions to the Study of Freud's *Interpretation of Dreams*. *J. Amer. Psychoanal. Assn.*, 2:180-191.

———(1956), On Some Vicissitudes of Insight in Psychoanalysis. *Internat. J. Psycho-Anal.*, 37:445-455.

Lehmann, H. (1966), Two Dreams and a Childhood Memory of Freud. *J. Amer. Psychoanal. Assn.*, 14:388-405.

Lewin, B. D. (1952), Phobic Symptoms and Dream Interpretation. In: *Selected Writings*. New York: Psychoanalytic Quarterly, Inc., 1973, pp. 187-212.

_____(1953), The Forgetting of Dreams. In: *Drives, Affects and Behavior*, ed. R. M. Loewenstein. New York: International Universities Press, pp. 191-202.

_____(1955), Dream Psychology and the Analytic Situation. In: *Selected Writings*. New York: Psychoanalytic Quarterly, Inc., 1973, pp. 264-290.

_____(1969), Remarks on Creativity, Imagery, and the Dream. In: *Selected Writings*. New York: Psychoanalytic Quarterly, Inc., 1973, pp. 173-183.

Lincoln, J. S. (1935), *The Dream in Primitive Cultures*. London: Cresset Press.

Lippman, H. S. (1945), The Use of Dreams in Psychiatric Work with Children. *The Psychoanalytic Study of the Child*, 1:233-245. New York: International Universities Press.

Loewenstein, R. (1949), A Posttraumatic Dream. *Psychoanal. Quart.*, 18:449-454.

_____(1951), The Problem of Interpretation. *Psychoanal. Quart.*, 20:1-13.

Loomis, E. A., Jr. (1956), A Rare Detail in the Dreams of Two Patients. *J. Amer. Psychoanal. Assn.*, 4:53-55.

Lorand, S. & Feldman, S. (1955), The Symbolism of Teeth in Dreams. *Internat. J. Psycho-Anal.*, 36:145-161.

Mack, J. E. (1970), *Nightmares and Human Conflict*. Boston: Little, Brown.

Niederland, W. G. (1957a), River Symbolism. *Psychoanal. Quart.*, 25:469-504, 26:50-72.

_____(1957b), The Earliest Dreams of a Young Child. *The Psychoanalytic Study of the Child*, 12:190-208. New York: International Universities Press.

Pollack, G. H. & Muslin, H. L. (1962), Dreams During Surgical Procedures. *Psychoanal. Quart.*, 31:175-202.

Rangell, L., reporter (1956), Panel on "The Dream in the Practice of Psychoanalysis." *J. Amer. Psychoanal. Assn.*, 4:122-137.

Renneker, R. (1952), Dream Timing. *Psychoanal. Quart.*, 21:81-91.

Róheim, G. (1952), *The Gates of the Dream*. New York: International Universities Press.

Saul, L. J. (1953), The Ego in a Dream. *Psychoanal. Quart.*, 22:257-258.

_____(1966), Embarrassment Dreams of Nakedness. *Internat. J. Psycho-Anal.*, 47:552-558.

_____(1967), Dream Form and Strength of Impulse in Dreams of

Falling and Other Dreams of Descent. *Internat. J. Psycho-Anal.*, 48:281-287.

Sharpe, E. F. (1949), *Dream Analysis*. London: Hogarth Press.

Shengold, L. (1966), The Metaphor of the Journey in *The Interpretation of Dreams. Amer. Imago*, 23:316-331.

Snyder, F. (1963), The New Biology of Dreaming. *Arch. Gen. Psychiat.*, 8:381-391.

Spanjaard, J. (1969), The Manifest Dream Content and Its Significance for the Interpretation of Dreams. *Internat. J. Psycho-Anal.*, 50:221-235.

Steiner, M. (1937), The Dream Symbolism of the Analytic Situation. *Internat. J. Psycho-Anal.*, 18:294-305.

Sterba, R. (1928), An Examination Dream. *Internat. J. Psycho-Anal.*, 9:353-354.

———(1946), Dreams and Acting Out. *Psychoanal. Quart.*, 15:175-179.

Stewart, H. (1973), The Experiencing of the Dream and the Transference. *Internat. J. Psycho-Anal.*, 54:345-347.

Waelder, R., reporter (1949), Panel on "Dream Theory and Interpretation." *Bull. Amer. Psychoanal. Assn.*, 5:36-40.

Waldhorn, H. F. (1967), The Place of the Dream in Clinical Psychoanalysis. *Kris Study Group Monogr.*, 2:96-105. New York: International Universities Press.

Whitman, R. M. (1963), Remembering and Forgetting Dreams in Psychoanalysis. *J. Amer. Psychoanal. Assn.*, 11:752-774.

——— Kramer, M., & Baldridge, B. J. (1969), Dreams About the Patient. *J. Amer. Psychoanal. Assn.*, 17:702-727.

Winterstein, A. (1954), A Typical Dream Sensation and Its Meaning. *Internat. J. Psycho-Anal.*, 35:229-233.

INDICES

Index of Dreams

275

Index

279